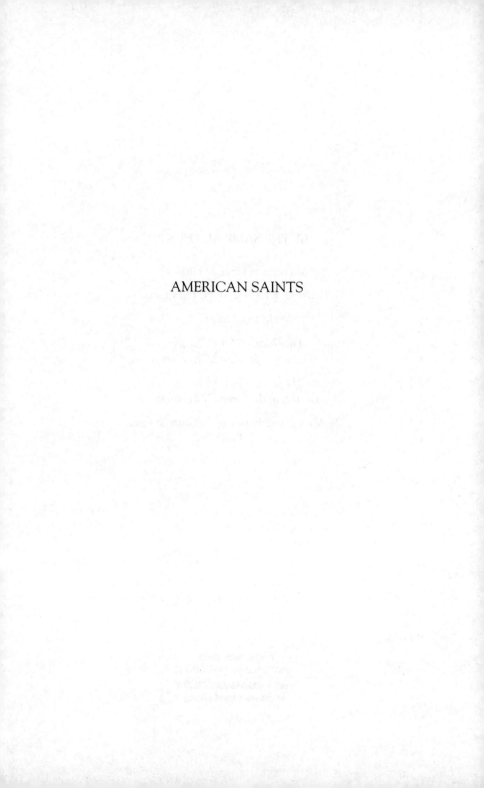

AMERICAN SAINTS

BY THE SAME AUTHOR

Moments in Catholic History

Traveling With Jesus in the Holy Land

Married Saints

The Doctors of the Church:
Doctors of the First Millennium

The Doctors of the Church:
Doctors of the Second Millennium

The Mission and Future of the Catholic Press
(Editor)

American Saints

*Five Centuries of Heroic Sanctity
on the American Continents*

JOHN F. FINK

ALBA·HOUSE   NEW·YORK

SOCIETY OF ST. PAUL, 2187 VICTORY BLVD., STATEN ISLAND, NEW YORK 10314

ST PAULS

Library of Congress Cataloging-in-Publication Data

Fink, John F.
    American saints: five centuries of heroic sanctity on the American
continents / John F. Fink
        p. cm.
    ISBN 0-8189-0900-5 (alk. paper)
    1. Christian saints—America.   I. Title.

BX4659.A 45 F56 2001
282'.092'273—dc21
[B]   2001033317

Produced and designed in the United States of America by the
Fathers and Brothers of the Society of St. Paul,
2187 Victory Boulevard, Staten Island, New York 10314-6603,
as part of their communications apostolate.

ISBN: 0-8189-0900-5

Printing Information:

Current Printing - first digit	1	2	3	4	5	6	7	8	9	10

Year of Current Printing - first year shown

2001	2002	2003	2004	2005	2006	2007	2008	2009	2010

DEDICATION

To our grandchildren:

Jacklyn
Angela
Brian
Hilary
Jack
Joseph
Hannah
Claire
Tyler
David

May you all become American saints

Table of Contents

Introduction

By my count, 137 people who have lived on the American continents have been beatified or canonized by the Roman Catholic Church. Sixty have been canonized and 77 have been beatified. I say "by my count" because there doesn't seem to be an official list. When Archbishop José Saraiva Martins, the prefect of the Vatican's Congregation for the Causes of Saints, sent me a list of "Saints and Blesseds of the American Continents," he said in his letter that it was an "unofficial list." I did indeed discover some other saints and blesseds that I thought should be included.

For the record, as of the beginning of the year 2001, those 137 saints and blesseds lived in fifteen countries of the Americas. Fifty were from Mexico and 33 were from Brazil. Both Canada and the United States can claim eight North American martyrs. Twelve more saints or blesseds were from Canada and nine more were from the United States. Seven were from Peru, three were from Colombia, three were from Ecuador, three were from Paraguay, two were from Argentina, two were from Chile, one was from Guatemala, one was from Cuba, one was from the Dominican Republic, one was from Uruguay, and one was from Venezuela.

Why include blesseds—those who have "only" been beatified — in a book called *American Saints*? Because we can certainly be sure that those who have made it to that step, just below canonization, are truly in heaven. Their lives have been investigated thoroughly and, except in the case of martyrs, the Catholic Church has certified at least one miracle worked by God through their in-

tercession. Furthermore, after a person is beatified, he or she is usually assigned a feast day in the liturgical calendar.

In most cases, though not all, it is simply a matter of time
before blesseds will be canonized. It seems to me that, with some
exceptions, all the blesseds included in this book will eventually
be canonized. The exceptions are Blessed Sebastian Aparicio, who
was beatified in 1789, and ten Mexican martyrs who were beatified
in 1867. It seems that, if they were going to be canonized, it would
have happened long before now.

Except for Sebastian Aparício and those ten Mexican martyrs, all the blesseds in this book were beatified between 1980 and
2000.

All except eight of the saints in this book were canonized
during the twentieth century or in 2000 (arguably still part of the
twentieth century). The exceptions are Saints Rose of Lima,
Turibius de Mogrovejo, and Francis Solano, all of Peru; Peter
Claver of Colombia; and five Mexicans who were martyred in
Nagasaki, Japan.

One of those martyrs, Philip of Jesús de las Casas, was the
first native of the Americas eventually to become a canonized saint
when Pope Pius IX canonized him in 1862. Philip was born in 1572
and died in 1597. However, when Juan Diego, who has been
beatified, is canonized, he will be the first native-born saint since
he was born in 1474. The first native-born person to be canonized, though, was Rose of Lima, canonized in 1671.

Surprisingly, at least to me, is the fact that Saint Katharine
Drexel, canonized on October 1, 2000, is the only native-born citi-
zen of the United States to be canonized or beatified. Kateri
Tekakwitha is the first blessed to be born in what is now the United
States and Elizabeth Ann Seton was also born in what is now the
United States, but both were born before the United States be-
came a separate country. The other U.S. saints and blesseds were
all born outside of the United States.

Since one of my previous books was *Married Saints* (published
by Alba House), I was interested in the number of American saints

and blesseds who were married. Saint Elizabeth Ann Seton of the United States, Saint Marie Marguerite d'Youville and Blessed Marie of the Incarnation of Canada, and Blessed Juan Diego and Saint Manuel Morales of Mexico were all married at some time in their lives. Of those five, only Saint Manuel Morales was married at the time of his death; the other four were widowed. In addition, some of the thirty Brazilian martyrs who were beatified on March 5, 2000 were married.

This is not the first book about the saints of the American continents. While I was president and publisher of Our Sunday Visitor, we published in 1974 the book *Saints of the Americas*, by Rev. M.A. Habig, O.F.M. It too profiled those who had been beatified as well as those who had been canonized. I used that book as one of my sources for some of the saints. However, at the time it was published, there were only 45 saints and blesseds from the American continents—22 saints and 23 blesseds. This gives an idea of how many people from the Americas Pope John Paul II has beatified or canonized.

Pope John Paul has indeed beatified and canonized many more people than any of his predecessors. Between the time I proposed this book to the editors at Alba House in January of 2000 and the time it was published, the pope canonized 28 people from the Americas and beatified 32.

All of which makes me believe that soon this book might be as out-of-date as the one Father Habig wrote in 1974. I suspect that Pope John Paul, or possibly his successor, will soon canonize both Blessed Juan Diego and Blessed Miguel Agustín Pro of Mexico, and surely Cardinal Terence Cooke, Capuchin Father Solanus Casey, and Pierre Toussaint, all from the United States, aren't too far away from beatification.

This book obviously is not as large as it could be. None of the chapters are intended to be complete biographies, but only profiles of some of America's saints. I could also have written separate chapters about some of the saints mentioned only briefly in the final chapter, but chose not to because we did not want the book to be too long. I simply used my best judgment about which saints and blesseds to write profiles about and which to mention briefly in the final chapter. I apologize to those who supplied me with a great deal of information about a particular saint or blessed and I decided not to devote an entire chapter to him or her.

I want to thank the many people who helped with this book by supplying information for me. They include Archbishop José Martins, prefect of the Congregation for the Causes of Saints, who supplied the "unofficial list"; Archbishop John P. Foley, president of the Pontifical Council for Social Communications, for putting me in touch with Archbishop Martins; and Gloria Garcia at the Mexican Bishops Conference, who was invaluable for supplying information about all fifty of the Mexicans.

Also, Tom Lorsung, editor-in-chief, and Katherine Nuss, librarian, at Catholic News Service in Washington for supplying past news articles about canonizations and beatifications; Bernard Daly in Ottawa, who forwarded a list of all Canadian saints and blesseds; and Father Paul Quinter, editor of *The Catholic Standard and Times* of Philadelphia, for his help with profiles of Saints John Neumann and Katharine Drexel.

Also the following shrines and religious orders who sent information about various saints and blesseds: Shrine of the North American Martyrs, Auriesville, New York; National Shrine of Blessed Kateri Tekakwitha, Fonda, New York; Sisters of Charity of Montreal; National Shrine of Saint Elizabeth Ann Seton, Emmitsburg, Maryland; Mission San Carlos, Carmel, California; Marie-Rose Center, Longueuil, Quebec; Memorial Shrine of Saint Rose Philippine Duchesne, St. Charles, Missouri; Sisters of Providence, Saint Mary-of-the-Woods, Indiana; Saint John Neumann Shrine, Philadelphia, Pennsylvania; Perpetual Help Confraternity, Chicago, Illinois; Seelos Center and Shrine, New Orleans, Louisiana; Shrine of Saint Frances Xavier Cabrini, New York; Saint Joseph's Oratory, Montreal, Quebec; Sisters of the Blessed Sacrament, Bensalem, Pennsylvania; Centre d'animation François-de-Laval, Quebec; Sisters of Saint Joseph of Saint Hyacinthe, Quebec; Little Sisters of the Holy Family, Sherbrooke, Quebec; Centre Frederic Jansoone, Troi-Rivieres, Quebec; and the Religious of Jesus and Mary, Sillery, Quebec.

Finally, I used the book *Molokai: The Story of Father Damien* (published by Alba House) as my source for the chapter on Blessed Damien de Veuster.

AMERICAN SAINTS

CHAPTER I

Blessed Juan Diego

(1474-1548)

The conquest of the indigenous people who inhabited the American continents followed closely behind the discovery of America by Christopher Columbus in 1492. Hernando Cortés and his soldiers arrived in Mexico in 1519 and were ruthless in their conquest of Mexico. Millions of natives died. However, missionaries soon arrived and they tried to convert, rather than conquer, the people who inhabited the New World.

Not counting the chaplains in Cortés's army, the first Franciscan missionaries arrived in New Spain in 1523. Six years later, Brother Peter of Ghent was able to report to his Belgian confreres that he and his companions had already baptized more than 200,000 natives and in 1531 Father Martin of Valencia reported that more than a million Indians had been converted. But that number increased by eight times during the next few years as the result of an amazing event that occurred in 1531. And that's where Blessed Juan Diego entered history.

Juan Diego was a simple Aztec Indian whose parents belonged to a lower but propertied class. He was born in 1474 in Cuauhtitlan, a village sixteen miles northwest of what is now Mexico City but was then known as Tenochtitlan. He was given the name

Cuauhtlatoatzin, which some reports say meant "the eagle who speaks" in the Nahuatl language and others say meant "he who relates the things of God." He was among the first Christian converts after the Franciscans arrived in 1523. He was baptized and received his new name, along with his wife, Maria Lucia, and his uncle, Juan Bernardino, when he was 48 years old. Maria Lucia died in 1529 and Juan Diego returned to live with his uncle, who had played the role of foster father from the time Juan Diego was a little boy.

Juan became a devout Catholic who tried to get to Mass as often as possible at the Church of Santiago el Mayor (James the Greater) in Tolpetlac, a mission settlement. That's where he was going on the morning of Saturday, December 9, 1531. It was to be a special Mass for the feast of the Immaculate Conception, which was observed on that date in those days. As he reached the top of a hill called Tepeyac, he first heard beautiful music and then saw a beautiful lady who called his name: "Juanito, Juan Diegito, where are you going?"

After Juan replied that he was going to church, the lady identified herself as "the ever-Virgin Mary, the Mother of the true God, who is the author of life, who is the creator of all things and Lord of heaven and earth." She then said that she wanted a chapel to be built there in which "I will demonstrate, I will manifest, I will give all my love, my compassion, my help and my protection to the people."

She made it clear that she wanted the chapel built on Tepeyac hill, the site of a shrine to the Aztec goddess Tonantzin, mother of all native gods in central Mexico.

Juan Diego promised to do what he could and hurried south to Tenochtitlan (Mexico City) to see Fray Juan de Zumarraga, the Franciscan priest who had been appointed bishop but who had not yet been consecrated. He was to become a great force for good over the next 25 years, introducing into the New World the first library, hospital, college and printing press. He listened to the 57-year-old Juan Diego, though with considerable doubt, as anyone might do when someone says he or she has seen a vision of Mary. He thought it prudent to withhold judgment for the time being.

Juan Diego was disappointed that the bishop did not believe him. He returned to Tepeyac hill, sure that the lady would be there. She was. Juan told her sadly that, although the bishop had listened to him attentively, he knew that he did not believe him. Juan told the lady that it would be better if she sent someone else to the bishop—"one of the noblemen who are well known, revered and respected"—so that her words would be believed.

Mary replied, saying, "It is true that I do not lack servants or ambassadors to whom I could entrust my message so that my will could be fulfilled. But it is important that you speak for me in this matter." She asked him to try again and Juan promised that he would return to the hill the next day around sunset to report the bishop's answer.

The next day was Sunday. Juan attended Mass in the morning and then returned to the bishop's residence. Since it was a Sunday, the bishop's servants tried to turn him away and it was only with great persistence that he finally was allowed to see Bishop Zumarraga. Juan fell on his knees and begged the bishop to listen to the message sent by the Blessed Virgin. At first the bishop was severe with Juan, telling him that he had only his word for what was being requested. But eventually he told Juan to bring him some sign from the lady that would convince him of her request.

Juan met Mary at the time appointed and gave his report. She promised to have a sign for him the next day. "Do not forget me," she told Juan.

Juan didn't forget, but he also didn't meet the lady the next day. When he got home on Sunday night he found his uncle, Juan Bernardino, seriously sick with a fever that was usually fatal for the Indians. Juan Diego spent all day Monday caring for his sick uncle, whose condition worsened on Monday night. Juan Bernardino's condition was so bad that Juan Diego thought he had better get a priest to give his uncle the last sacraments.

That's what he had in mind on Tuesday morning, December

12, when he hurried to the mission settlement. He even tried to avoid the possibility of meeting the Virgin by taking a different route. It didn't work. The lady met him again and asked, "Where are you going, least of my sons? And what road is this you are taking?"

Embarrassed, Juan explained that his uncle "is very sick with an illness so acute that without doubt he will die of it. I am hurrying to your house in Mexico to call one of Our Lord's dear ones, our priests, to come to hear his confession and prepare him for death. Then I will come back here to this place to obey your command."

Mary replied, "Am I not here who am your mother? Are you not under my shadow and protection? Am I not your fountain of life? Are you not in the fold of my mantle, in the crossing of my arms? Do not be troubled or take thought of your uncle's illness, for he will not die of this. He is well already. Do you need anything else?"

Without hesitation, Juan believed the Virgin and said that he would go straight to the bishop with whatever sign she had for him. Mary told him to go to the top of the hill and to cut the roses he would find there, gather them in his tilma (a cloak made from the fibers of a cactus plant), and bring them to her. Although there had never been roses at the top of Tepeyac hill, especially in December, Juan found them there. He cut them and brought them to Mary, who carefully rearranged them in his tilma. She then instructed him to take them to the bishop.

For the third time, Juan Diego went to Bishop-elect Zumarraga's home. Once more the servants there showed their unhappiness at seeing him again and made him wait for a long time. Finally, though, they told the bishop that the pesky Indian was there again and seemed to be hiding flowers in his tilma. The bishop agreed to see him.

Juan Diego explained what had happened since the two last met, including Mary's instructions to cut the roses at the top of Tepeyac hill. "Although I knew very well," he said, "that the hilltop was not a place for flowers, since it is a place of thorns, cactuses, stones and mesquites, I was not confused and did not doubt her. When I reached the summit, I saw there was a garden with many fragrant flowers."

He then opened his tilma to show the bishop the flowers. As he did so, Bishop Zumarraga fell to his knees because there on Juan's tilma was a large painting of the Lady of Tepeyac hill. Begging forgiveness for doubting Juan, the bishop untied the knot of the tilma behind Juan's neck, carried the full-length picture of Mary to his chapel, and hung it on the wall.

Bishop Zumarraga invited Juan to stay with him overnight and then to show him exactly where Mary wanted her church to be built. The next day, after doing that, Juan was anxious to get home to see how his uncle was. He found Juan Bernardino fully recovered and eager to tell his part of the story. He said that the lady had also appeared to him at exactly the time that she told Juan Diego that Juan Bernardino was well.

Mary also revealed to the 73-year-old Juan Bernardino the name she wanted to be called: Our Lady of Guadalupe. This is the Arabic name for the site of a monastery in Spain and it is believed that Mary probably said something to Juan Bernardino in the Nahuatl language that sounded like Guadalupe. Perhaps she called herself *Hehuatzin ni Goatlaxupeuh* which means "I am she who crushed the serpent." The sounds of the last word and of Guadalupe are similar. The Indians, though, continued to refer to the Virgin as Tonantzin until well into the seventeenth century.

Bishop Zumarraga immediately ordered the construction of a chapel to house Juan Diego's tilma. It was built quickly and the painting was moved there the day after Christmas, 1531. The small chapel was enlarged in 1557, a basilica was built in 1709 and a new basilica was completed in 1976.

The fact that Juan Diego's tilma continues to hang there today must be considered a miracle in itself. It was made of fibers from the maguey cactus plant, a material that resembles burlap and would normally deteriorate in twenty or thirty years. Yet today it shows no signs of deterioration. It also is not suitable for a painting, since it has no sizing to stiffen it in preparation for receiving pigment. No artist would have chosen it for such a purpose. Furthermore, artists who have examined it closely cannot explain why the colors in the image show no sign of fading. They remain as brilliant as ever. Moreover, the colors do not penetrate the threads of the cloth, but lie on top of it like the emulsion of a photographic print. The conclusion is that the image can be nothing short of miraculous.

The Indians saw in Juan Diego's tilma a catechism leading them to the true God. The image of the lady with the robes she wore, the angel below her, the moon she stood on, the other details in the painting, all had a meaning for the natives. From then on, virtually the entire Indian population converted to Catholicism. It was especially significant to the Indians that the Mother of God chose a humble Indian peasant to spread the faith of the people who had conquered them.

As for Juan Diego, after the first chapel was built, he gave his little house and the few cornfields that he owned to his uncle and went to live in a one-room adobe hut next to the chapel. He lived alone but delighted in telling the story of the apparitions to everyone who visited the chapel. He died there in 1548 at age 74 and was buried at the base of Tepeyac hill.

His cause for beatification was officially opened on June 26, 1981 and he was beatified on April 9, 1990. At that time the Church recognized that generations of Catholics had established a cult to Juan Diego. His feast day is observed in the Americas on December 9. The feast of Our Lady of Guadalupe is celebrated on December 12. In 1754 Pope Benedict XIV named Mary the patroness of New Spain. Our Lady of Guadalupe was designated patroness of Latin America by Pope Pius X in 1910 and of the Americas by Pope Pius XII in 1945.

As this book goes to press it is expected that the pope will announce a date soon for Juan Diego's canonization.

CHAPTER 2

Five Peruvian Saints
(1538-1645)

The country of Peru in South America claims five canonized saints, all of whom lived and died there in the sixteenth and seventeenth centuries. One of them, though, Saint Francis Solano, is also rightly claimed by Argentina and Paraguay, countries in which he carried on missionary work. Two blesseds from Peru are included in the final chapter of this book.

Saint Turibius de Mogrovejo
(1538-1606)

The Spanish Inquisition would seem an unlikely place to produce a Peruvian saint, but it did. Turibius (or Toribio) Alfonso de Mogrovejo y Robles was a brilliant scholar and a doctor of both civil and canon law in Spain. He eventually became a professor of law at the University of Salamanca and then was appointed chief judge of the Inquisition at Granada. During the five years he held that position, he earned a reputation as a just judge, a father and counselor, and protector of the innocent.

The first bishop of Lima, Peru, Archbishop Jerónimo Loaysa, died in 1575 and King Philip II looked for a successor. He concluded that there was no one more qualified than Turibius. The problem was that Turibius was a layman who had no interest in being bishop of the Spanish colony in the New World. He cited canons that forbade giving laymen ecclesiastical honors and pleaded that he was unqualified for the office. The king persisted, though, and Turibius discerned that it was God's will that he should acquiesce. He was ordained a priest in 1578 and consecrated a bishop in 1580.

Bidding his aged mother good-bye, Turibius left Spain in 1580 but didn't arrive in Peru until May 24, 1581. At this time, Peru included modern Ecuador and Bolivia. Turibius's ship docked 600 miles from Lima and he made the rest of the trip by foot, stopping all along the way to give instructions and administer the sacraments.

Arriving in Lima, he found appalling conditions. Colonialism was at its worst. The Spanish conquistadors were oppressing the indigenous people. He also found abuses among the clergy, who lived openly with women. When some of the clergy tried to excuse themselves by appealing to longstanding tradition, Turibius quoted the words of Tertullian: "Christ said, 'I am the truth'; he did not say, 'I am the custom.' "

Turibius worked among the poor people of Peru for 26 years. He studied the dialects of the Quechua language in order to serve the native people as a true father, protector, and benefactor.

Shortly after his arrival in Lima, Archbishop Turibius convoked a provincial council, the Third Council of Lima. It concerned itself primarily with the work of civilizing and Christianizing the Indians and with the relations of the Spanish settlers with the Indians. Turibius presided over other councils in 1591 and 1601. He also decided that his archdiocese should have a synod every two years and over time he conducted thirteen of them.

He also made pastoral visitations to every part of his vast diocese, and it has been estimated that he traveled 18,000 miles—on foot or muleback—to do it. He instructed converts, baptized and confirmed them. One of those to whom he administered the sacrament of confirmation was Saint Rose of Lima.

Archbishop Turibius died while on one of his visitations—in Sana, 110 miles from Lima—on March 23, 1606. Pope Innocent XI beatified him in 1679 and Pope Benedict XIII canonized him in 1726. His feast is celebrated on March 23.

Saint Francis Solano
(1549-1610)

Perhaps Saint Francis Solano (or Solanus) should be the patron saint of violinists because he used a homemade violin in his missionary work. It is said that the indigenous people of South America were attracted by the sweet strains of his violin along with the hymns he sang with a melodious voice.

Francis had already made a name for himself in his native Spain well before he came to the Americas. Born in 1549, he joined the Franciscans when he was twenty and was ordained a priest at age 27. He made his reputation as a great preacher, but also for his selfless work among the sick when a pestilence broke out in Andalusia in 1583. When the plague ended, the grateful people tried to heap honors on Francis but, to avoid them, he asked his superior to transfer him to Granada.

Around this time, the Franciscans were asked to supply more missionaries for the New World, and Francis was chosen for the mission fields of Tucumán in northern Argentina. The voyage was arduous. It included stopping on the island of Española (Haiti and the Dominican Republic), crossing the Isthmus of Panama on foot, and a shipwreck in which 130 passengers were drowned. Francis was among survivors who made it to shore, but they were stranded there for fifty days before another ship arrived. Finally Francis and his fellow missionaries reached Lima, Peru, but stayed there only a few days before trekking 1,400 miles across the Andes and south to Tucumán. He arrived in 1590.

Francis learned the Indian languages and began his work among the natives. He had lost his violin in the shipwreck, but made a new one with only two strings. His playing and singing soothed the Indians and soon he achieved remarkable results. His converts ran into the thousands; one biographer even said hundreds of thousands.

Francis was appointed custodian, or superior, of the Custody of Tucumán in 1595 and spent the next six years traveling almost constantly from one mission to another, not only in Argentina but also in neighboring Paraguay. Whenever possible, he played the role of peacemaker between the Indians and the Spanish settlers.

He was also credited for pacifying and converting 9,000 hostile Indians with a single sermon. During Maundy Thursday services at an Indian village, the hostile Indians arrived and threatened an attack. Francis confronted them and invited them to abandon the law of hatred and embrace that of love. Although the Indians spoke different dialects, all were able to understand Francis and declared themselves ready to adopt the Christian way of life.

In 1601, after eleven years among the Indians of Tucumán, Francis was reassigned to a house of recollection in Lima, Peru. The rest of his life was spent in Peru, preaching mainly to the Spaniards there. He died in Lima on July 14, 1610 at age 59. Pope Clement X beatified him in 1675 and Pope Benedict XIII canonized him in 1726. His feast is celebrated on July 14.

Saint Martin de Porres
(1579-1639)

Saint Martin de Porres was one of those individuals whose sanctity was widely recognized during their lifetime. Not only was he known for spending long hours in prayer and for imposing on himself rigorous penances, but also miraculous things happened in his presence. Sick people were suddenly cured, food for the poor multiplied, trees that he planted bore fruit throughout the year, and he was seen in two different places at the same time. Martin was a poor mulatto, with only a rudimentary education, who was happy to do the most menial of jobs. Yet learned men often consulted him because of his expert theological knowledge.

Martin was born in Lima, Peru on December 9, 1579, the illegitimate son of a Spanish grandee, Don Juan de Porres, and a black woman from Panama named Anna Velásquez. His father was disappointed that Martin and his sister Juana were both as black as their mother and had similar features. After he was named governor of Panama, Don Juan abandoned his family and Martin was reared in poverty in Lima. When he was twelve, his mother apprenticed him to a barber-surgeon so he could learn a trade.

When he was fifteen, the Blessed Virgin appeared to Martin and instructed him to enter the Dominican friary of the Most Holy Rosary in Lima. He went to the friary and asked to be admitted as a tertiary brother, or lay helper, not feeling worthy to ask to become a friar. He was admitted. Nine years later, when he was 24, because he had earned a reputation for extraordinary holiness, his superiors asked him to become a Dominican friar. He took his vows on June 2, 1603.

Martin worked as the friary's infirmarian, barber, tailor, and distributor of funds to the poor. Recognizing his devotion to the needy, wealthy citizens of Lima gave him large sums of money with which he was able to found an orphanage for several hundred children. He cared especially for slaves brought to Lima from Africa, not because they were black as he was but because they were the most neglected and needed the most help. When a new ship of slaves arrived, he would meet it, tend to the sick, and instruct the slaves about Christianity.

Once when his priory was deeply in debt, Martin told his superiors, "I am only a poor mulatto. Sell me. I am the property of the order. Sell me."

Martin's solicitude extended not only to his fellow men and women, but also to animals, even vermin. He established a refuge and hospital for cats and dogs at his sister's home, and he laid out food for rats. He told owners of granaries that he had told the rats not to eat their grain so there was no need to kill them. The rats didn't.

Martin was a friend of two of the other saints from Lima. He was six years older than John Masias and seven years older than Rose.

Martin devoted 45 years of his life to the poor of Lima. After his death on November 4, 1639, one month before his sixtieth birthday, the entire city mourned his passing. Rich and poor alike attended his funeral.

Pope Gregory XVI beatified him in 1837 and Pope John XXIII canonized him on May 6, 1962. His feast is celebrated on November 3.

Saint Rose of Lima
(1586-1617)

Saint Rose of Lima is called the first American-born saint because she was the first person born in the Americas to be canonized. However, she is not the first saint to be born in the New World because Saint Philip (or Felipe) of Jesus was born in Mexico seventeen years before Saint Rose and Saint Roch González of Paraguay was born ten years before her.

She was born in 1586 to Don Gaspar de Flores and his wife, María de Oliva, and given the name Isabel after her grandmother. However, an Indian maid named Mariana looked at the baby in her cradle and said, "Our beautiful baby looks just like a rose." From then on she was called Rose (except by her grandmother).

Rose displayed an extraordinary love for God even as a child. As soon as she was old enough to read, she read a book about Saint Catherine of Siena and decided to pattern her own life after that of Saint Catherine. When she was only six she began to fast three times a week, taking only bread and water.

Rose's family moved from Lima to Quives, about fifty miles away, when her father was appointed superintendent of the silver mines there. She was there when Archbishop Turibius passed through on his last pastoral visitation to his vast diocese, and he administered the sacrament of confirmation to Rose. She was eleven at the time.

After three years in Quives, the mining venture apparently failed and the Flores family moved back into their large home in Lima. Rose helped to support the family by working in the vegetable garden and through her needlework, making exquisite lace and embroidered silks.

As she approached marriageable age, Rose's parents began to make arrangements for an advantageous marriage for her, but Rose refused to consider it. She took a vow of virginity and deliberately tried to make herself less attractive by rubbing pepper on her face. She had to struggle with her parents for ten years over the marriage issue.

Her parents refused to allow her to enter a convent, so when she was twenty Rose joined the Third Order of Saint Dominic, taking the name Rose of Saint Mary. She continued to live a life of penance and built for herself a small hut, only five by four feet, in her garden where she lived in solitude, prayer and contemplation. She began to wear a crown of thorns, a thin circlet of silver studded on the inside with little sharp prickles.

Rose also combined her life as a recluse with an active apostolate of charity. With her mother's consent, she converted some rooms in her home where she cared for homeless children, the elderly and the sick. This was the beginning of social services in Peru.

Eventually, Rose's eccentric life came to the attention of the Court of the Inquisition. Some eminent theologians examined her and concluded that her holiness was genuine and that God had endowed her with infused knowledge on the subject of ascetical theology and the spiritual life.

During the last three years of Rose's life she lived in a small attic room in the home of Don Gonzalo and Doña María Maza. The Mazas invited her to instruct their daughters, Micaela and Andrea. What mainly attracted Rose, though, was the fact that the Mazas had a chapel in their home.

Rose was credited with saving the city of Lima three times. In 1615, the Dutch pirate George Spitberg and his men invaded Lima. Rose hurried to the Church of Santo Domingo and stood in front of the tabernacle as the pirates entered the church. The pirates fled back to their ships and abandoned their plan to plunder the city. The other two occasions when her prayers were thought to have saved the city were when Indians rose in widespread rebellion but did not invade Lima, and when earthquakes in the vicinity did not damage Lima.

Her penances had weakened her health and she suffered acute pains on August 1, 1617. Her body became rigid and she suffered great pain before she died at midnight on August 23-24, 1617. She was only 31 years old. During her funeral prominent men of the city took turns carrying her coffin.

Pope Clement X beatified Rose in 1668. A year later he declared Blessed Rose of Saint Mary to be the patron of Latin America and the Philippines. In 1671, the same pope canonized her. Her feast is celebrated on August 23.

Saint John Masias
(1585-1645)

Saint John Masias (also spelled John de Massias and John Macias) was a contemporary and friend of Saint Martin de Porres. Both were Dominican brothers although they belonged to different priories in Lima, Peru. John, though, was not born in Lima, as Martin was.

John was born in the Villa de Rivera, Estremadura, Spain, in 1586, the son of Pedro Masias de Arcos and Inés Sánchez. They instilled in their son a deep longing for sanctity and, even as a little boy, John enjoyed praying in solitude more than playing with other children his age. His life with his parents, though, was short, because they both died when John was only four, and John was thereafter cared for by his uncle.

The uncle made John work as a shepherd. During the long hours tending the sheep, John learned the art of meditation and contemplation. He prayed the entire fifteen decades of the rosary—not only once a day but three times. It was a practice that he continued for the rest of his life. He developed particular devotion both to the Blessed Virgin and to Saint John the Evangelist.

When he was 34, John suddenly decided to go to the Spanish colonies in the New World. He said later that Saint John the Evangelist had appeared to him and told him to go to Lima, Peru, promising always to be his protector.

It took forty days for his ship to cross the Atlantic and land in Cartagena, Colombia. Saint Peter Claver was in Cartagena at the time (see next chapter), but there is no evidence that the two saints ever met. From Cartagena, John traveled by foot, canoe or boat to Quito, Ecuador, and from there, by foot or mule, to Lima. The actual journey from Cartagena to Lima took more than four months, but John interrupted it to work for two years on a cattle ranch because he had run out of money.

Upon arriving in Lima, John applied for admission in the priory of Saint Mary Magdalene. He was admitted as a brother and clothed with the Dominican habit on January 23, 1622, when he was 37.

Like some other saints in this book, John imposed penances upon himself that were sometimes imprudent, and his prior had to order him to moderate them. He tried to get by with only one hour of sleep at night while kneeling with his head on his bed. This resulted in a condition that required a painful operation to correct.

Brother John was the porter, or doorkeeper, at the priory for more than twenty years. In this capacity, he obtained food and clothing—sometimes in remarkable ways—for the poor who came to the priory. He fed more than 200 people daily, begging alms for that purpose from the city's wealthy. When he didn't have time to beg, he sent a burro through the city, the animal stopping at each home and, if not immediately noticed, knocking on the door with a leg. The people recognized the burro and would fill the pouches on its back.

He continued his devotions to the Blessed Virgin, particularly under her title of Nuestra Señora de Belén (Our Lady of Bethlehem). It was through his efforts, too, that the feast of the Holy Name of Mary began to be observed in a special way in Lima.

John died on September 17, 1645 at age sixty. Pope Gregory XVI beatified him in 1837 and Pope John Paul II canonized him in 1975. His feast is September 16.

CHAPTER 3

Saint Peter Claver

(1581-1654)

"The slave of the Negro slaves forever." That was the title Father Peter Claver claimed for himself during 35 years of active work among the slaves in Cartagena, on the coast of present-day Colombia.

African slave labor was introduced into the Americas, in Venezuela, as early as 1505, more than 100 years before Peter Claver arrived in the New World. Cartagena, Nueva Granada, founded in 1533, became one of the principal slave markets in the Americas because of its location on the Caribbean Sea. Here the slave dealers unloaded the slaves who had been sold to them by African chiefs on the coasts of Guinea before they were locked in the holds of ships. The slave dealers hardly cared that between a third and half of the slaves died during the six- or seven-week voyage. Upon arrival in Cartagena, the slaves were herded like cattle into sheds until they could be taken to the mines or plantations of their new owners.

By the early 1600's, as many as 1,000 slaves arrived in Cartagena every month, averaging 10,000 per year. Pope Paul III had condemned the slave trade and Pope Pius IX called it "supreme villainy," but that didn't seem to bother the Spanish slave dealers. The laws of Spain tried to ameliorate the slave trade somewhat, requiring that the slaves be allowed to become Christians and to enter into Christian marriages, forbidding the separation of members of families, and forbidding the seizure of slaves after they gained their freedom, but these laws were not always observed by the Spanish colonists. It often took men such as Peter Claver to see that they were observed.

Peter Claver was a contemporary of three of the saints of Lima, Peru. He was born in 1581, two years after Saint Martin de Porres, four years before Saint John Masias, and five years before Saint Rose of Lima. Indeed, Peter was serving the African slaves in Cartagena at the same time that Martin de Porres was doing so in Lima.

Peter was born near Barcelona, Spain, the son of a Catalonian farmer. He decided to become a priest and made his preparatory studies at the University of Barcelona. He then chose to become a Jesuit and was admitted to the novitiate at the age of twenty. After his novitiate, he spent a year in classical studies and then several years as a student of philosophy at the College of Montesion in Palma on the Spanish island of Mallorca.

When a group of missionaries was being recruited for Nueva Granada, Peter volunteered. He was selected and joined other missionaries who set sail from Spain for the New World in April of 1610. They landed at Cartagena and Peter went on to Santa Fe de Bogota to complete his theological studies. He was ordained a priest in Cartagena in 1615 and became the first priest to celebrate his first Mass in that city. Soon he began the work that was to consume the next 35 years of his life.

Peter was not the first Spanish priest to serve the black slaves in Catagena. His predecessor, Father Alfonso de Sandoval, had done it for forty years, and it was he who introduced Peter to this work. When the signal was sounded throughout the city that a ship with a load of slaves was entering the port, Peter went out on a pilot boat to meet it. He took with him food and medicines for the slaves who were in the worst condition. There wasn't much time for that, though, because the slaves were quickly herded out of the ships into the slave yards. There Peter distributed bread and other food, brandy, lemons, and tobacco. He went particularly to those with the most loathsome diseases that no one else would go near, bathed them, and gave them medicines.

"We must speak to them with our hands before we try to do so with our lips," Father Peter said. First he cared for the slaves' physical needs. Then he began to give them instructions in the Christian faith. With the help of seven interpreters (since the slaves came from various parts of Africa and spoke different dialects), Peter told the blacks that, though they were now slaves, they should still retain their dignity as human beings. Using pictures portraying the Crucifixion, he told them that Christ died for them as well as for the white man, and he gradually prepared them for baptism. It is claimed that Peter baptized 300,000 black slaves.

Once they were baptized, Peter continued to try to care for the slaves. Although most of them were marched to far-off mines and plantations and he never saw them again, he visited those who were nearby, preaching to them, praying with them, and trying to care for their physical needs. He made it a practice to lodge in the slave quarters rather than in the haciendas of the owners.

He also worked with the slave owners, trying to persuade them to live good Christian lives and to treat their slaves kindly. He pointed out that they contributed to their own temporal and spiritual good when they had regard for the temporal and spiritual well-being of their slaves. Some of the owners heeded his advice, others did not. The owners sometimes blamed him when some of the slaves got into trouble.

Taking care of the slaves, though, was only part of Father Peter's mission in Cartagena. He was the regular confessor for many of the people of the city, both blacks and whites. It is said that he sometimes spent as many as fifteen hours a day in the confessional and that he heard 5,000 confessions during his life. He also preached missions, not in a church but in the public square and in the countryside around Cartagena. He soon became known as "the apostle of all of Cartagena" and the citizens were convinced that his prayers averted divine punishments more than once. They believed that God had given Peter gifts of prophecy and other miracles.

There were two hospitals in Cartagena, one for general cases and the other for lepers. Peter visited both hospitals twice a week and many hardened sinners made their peace with God before their deaths because Father Peter was there to encourage them and pray with them. He also visited the prison regularly. During the 35 years of his active ministry, every condemned criminal had Peter Claver at his side during his execution, absolving him of his sins and praying for his soul.

Throughout his active ministry, Peter maintained a rigorous routine of penitential practices and long hours of prayer.

Near the end of his active life, Peter was accused of not taking proper care in the administration of the sacrament of baptism. Considering the large number of baptisms he had performed, undoubtedly some of the new converts were not ready for the sacrament. His superiors forbade him to baptize in the future. Peter submitted humbly.

The pope proclaimed the year 1650 a Jubilee Year and Peter Claver began a mission of preaching among the blacks along the coast. He was now 68 years old and his labors and personal penances, especially in the hot and humid climate of Cartagena, had weakened him. He had to give up his preaching and retire to his residence. When an epidemic broke out, he was one of the first victims. He managed to recover, but from then on he was too weak to continue his work. He was largely neglected and frequently was left helpless in his bed for days. However, he managed to rise from his bed in the summer of 1654 when Father Diego de Farina, appointed by the king of Spain to continue Peter's work, arrived. Peter was overjoyed to have a successor.

Peter remained ill and inactive for the last four years of his life. He died on September 8, 1654, the feast of the Nativity of the Blessed Virgin. The citizens of Cartagena—black and white, rich and poor—vied with one another to do him honor. He was buried with great pomp in front of the main altar of the church in Cartagena, where his body is still honored today. Pope Pius IX beatified him on July 16, 1850 and Pope Leo XIII canonized him on January 15, 1888. Pope Leo also proclaimed Saint Peter Claver to be the patron of all missionary enterprises among blacks throughout the world. His feast is celebrated on September 9.

CHAPTER 4

The North American Martyrs
(1593-1649)

While the Spanish were colonizing South America and Mexico, the French were in present-day Canada and the northern part of the United States. And just as Spanish Jesuit and Franciscan missionaries accompanied the Spanish conquistadors, so did French Jesuit and Franciscan missionaries accompany the French explorers. Some of the French missionaries paid with their lives. We know them as the eight North American Martyrs. However, the eight who are canonized saints were not the first missionaries to serve among the Indians in Canada and the United States. They weren't even the first martyrs.

The Jesuits first arrived in present-day Canada in 1611, establishing themselves in Acadia (Nova Scotia). They were there for only two years before the English drove them out. Meanwhile, Samuel de Champlain founded the city of Quebec in 1608 and he asked for missionaries. Franciscans arrived in 1615 and one of them, Father Joseph Le Caron, began to work among the Indians in Huronia, in the present province of Ontario. This is where the Huron Indians lived, although their real name was the Wyandots.

The Hurons, or Wyandots, were bitter enemies of the Iroquois, who were extremely ferocious and cruel. In 1619, one of the Franciscan missionaries, Father William Poullain, was captured by Iroquois and cruelly tortured. However, some Frenchmen managed to trade him for some Iroquois captives and thus saved his life. The first martyrs were Father Nicholas Viel and a newly baptized Indian who were thrown into the rapids of the St. Lawrence River near Montreal by Huron Indians in 1626. The first priest to preach to the Indians in New York was Franciscan Father Joseph de la Roche Dallion, who spent the fall and winter of 1627-28 in the western part of that state. Father de la Roche Dallion had come from France with five Jesuits in 1625.

Father John de Brébeuf was one of those Jesuits. He was born on March 25, 1593 near Lisieux, France. He entered the Jesuit novitiate at Rouen in 1617. However, he suffered from tuberculosis and was sent to complete his theological studies privately. He was thirty when he was ordained a priest. After that, he had a remarkable recovery and became a healthy, big and strong man.

He was 32 when he first went to New France. He spent two years among the Hurons, learning their language and their customs. Then, though, in 1629 the English seized the colony of New France and expelled all the missionaries. John was forced to return to France. The expulsion lasted for three years, until England gave New France back to France in 1632. Father de Brébeuf returned in 1633.

Before he returned, however, five other Jesuits arrived in New France. **Father Anthony Daniel** was one of them. He was born at Dieppe on May 27, 1601 and entered the Society of Jesus when he was twenty. He was ordained a priest ten years later and taught the classics at the College of Eu, where John de Brébeuf went after his expulsion from New France. Father Daniel left for New France in 1632.

Father Isaac Jogues and **Father Charles Garnier** arrived in 1636, **Father Noel Chabanel** in 1643, **Father Gabriel Lalemant** in 1646. We are not sure when **René Goupil** and **John de Lalande**, lay companions of Isaac Jogues, arrived.

Father Charles Garnier was a Parisian, son of wealthy parents. He was born on May 25, 1605 and entered the Society of Jesus when he was nineteen. He was a teacher at Eu from 1629 to 1632 and was ordained a priest in 1635. He offered to go to New France then, but his aged father, a generous benefactor of the Jesuits, was reluctant to see him go, and his departure was delayed for a year.

Father Gabriel Lalemant was born on October 10, 1610. He, too, was from Paris and was the nephew of two other prominent missionaries to New France, Fathers Charles and Jerome Lalemant. Gabriel didn't arrive in New France until 1646 because his health had been weak and he spent several years teaching in France.

Father Noel Chabanel was the youngest of the eight martyrs. Born in southern France on February 2, 1613, he joined the Jesuits in 1630 and after his studies taught for five years before traveling to New France in 1643.

Father Isaac Jogues was born in Orleans, France, on January 10, 1607, the son of a prominent official of that city. He graduated from college at the age of seventeen and then entered the Society of Jesus. He was ordained in 1636 and left for New France the same year. While he was in Quebec, Father Daniel arrived from Huronia with three Huron boys to begin a boarding school. Some Indians who had accompanied Father Daniel requested that a priest return with them. Father Jogues was selected.

After arriving in Huronia, and surviving an epidemic during which all six of the missionaries there almost died, Father Jogues began to learn the Indians' language. Father John de Brébeuf was his teacher. But the missionaries were encountering all kinds of difficulties with the Indians and things came to a head when the Indians held a council and condemned all the missionaries to death. Father de Brébeuf's knowledge of Indian customs came in handy, for he invited the Hurons to a farewell banquet, which they attended. He then spoke so convincingly about life after death that the Indians changed their mind about killing the missionaries and even adopted Father de Brébeuf into the tribe and made him a chief.

In 1638 a new mission was established with Father de Brébeuf in charge and Father Jogues his assistant. That year they baptized 72 adults and 48 children. The next few years were difficult ones, but the missionaries continued to make progress among the Indians. By the summer of 1642, though, they were in serious need of supplies and Father Jogues was chosen to go back to Quebec to get them. He left with eighteen Indians and five Frenchmen and, after 35 days of travel on foot and by canoe, arrived in Quebec.

After getting their supplies, a group of forty men, including 36 Hurons and four Frenchmen, began their return trip on August 1. On the second day they were suddenly attacked by a group of Iroquois Indians who had been waiting for them. Eighteen Hurons and the four Frenchmen were captured, while the rest of the Indians escaped into the forest.

The Iroquois Indians comprised five tribes—the Mohawks, Onondagas, Oneidas, Cayugas and Senecas—and it was a Mohawk war party that captured Father Jogues and his companions. For thirteen months they were led from village to village where they were beaten and tortured, and Father Jogues was forced to watch as his Huron converts were mangled and killed.

Father Jogues was a slave in a Mohawk village in Auriesville, New York on August 5, 1643, when he was permitted to write a detailed account of his captivity to his provincial superior in France. He wrote in Latin. He wrote that, after being taken prisoner, "The Mohawks grew fierce, and, assailing me with their fists and with knotty sticks, left me half dead on the ground; and, a little later… they also tore off my nails, and bit with their teeth my two forefingers, causing me incredible pain. They did the same to René Goupil [his lay assistant]."

During his 38 day journey with the Indians, he suffered other tortures: "They even went so far—a savage act—as to tear out in cold blood our hair and beards, and to wound us with their nails, which are extremely sharp, in the most tender and sensitive parts of the body."

Later, "They burned one of my fingers, and crushed another with their teeth. The others, already bruised and their sinews torn, they were so twisted that even at present, although partly healed, they are crippled and deformed." At the first of the Iroquois villages, "They beat us with sticks, fists, and stones. Two nails had been left me. These they tore out with their teeth, and tore off that flesh which is under them, with their very sharp nails, even to the bone."

At a second village, an Algonquin Christian woman was forced to cut off Father Jogues' left thumb and René Goupil's right thumb. Father Jogues wrote, "I thank God that they left me the one on my right hand, so that by this letter I may pray my fathers and brethren to offer prayers in the Holy Church of God."

At a third village, the Indians "threw coals and live ashes on our bare flesh, which for us who were bound, it was difficult to throw off."

After being taken from village to village and being tortured in new ways, the Indians killed René Goupil, the first of the eight martyrs to die. He was killed with a tomahawk after he made the Sign of the Cross on the brow of some children. Father Jogues wrote: "He was a man of unusual simplicity and innocence of life, of invincible patience, and very conformable to the will of God.... He had consecrated himself, under obedience to the superiors of the Society, in the service of our neophytes and catechumens.... The Sign of the Cross, which he often made on the brows of the children, was the last and true cause of his death."

Eventually Father Jogues was made a slave and his master granted him a certain measure of freedom. On July 31, 1643, he was taken along when the Indians went to Fort Orange (modern Albany, N.Y.) on a trading trip. While on the trip, he managed to escape with the help of the fort's commandant, hiding from the Indians behind some casks in the fort's storehouse. The commandant then offered the Indians a ransom of 300 livres of gold.

After the Indians had left, Father Jogues was taken by ship down the Hudson River to Manhattan Island and from there to England. He arrived back in France on Christmas Eve. He was welcomed with great respect as a living martyr. Pope Urban VIII granted him a dispensation that enabled to him to celebrate Mass with his mutilated hands, saying, "It would be shameful that a martyr of Christ be not allowed to drink the Blood of Christ."

Father Jogues could have remained in France, but his zeal led him back to his beloved Indians. After a few months, he was back in New France. In 1646, he went with John Bourdon, the government representative, to Ossernenon, the principal village of the Iroquois, to confer with the chiefs about a peace treaty. When he returned to Quebec, he left behind a box of religious objects, planning to return.

Shortly afterward, he returned to Iroquois country, this time with John de Lalande, his new lay assistant, thinking that the Indians would observe the new peace treaty. While he was gone, though, an epidemic had broken out among the Indians. Being superstitious, they blamed the epidemic on the box of religious objects Father Jogues had left behind. When he arrived at the Mohawk village of Auriesville, they again made him their prisoner. On October 18, 1646, as he entered a cabin for a meal to which the Indians had treacherously invited him, the Indians tomahawked him and cut off his head. The next day they killed John de Lalande.

Meanwhile, Father de Brébeuf and the other missionaries were experiencing considerable success among the Hurons. Father de Brébeuf composed catechisms and a dictionary in Huron and converted 7,000 Indians before his death. However, with the martyrdom of Father Jogues, the Iroquois made new efforts to destroy their enemies, the Hurons.

On July 4, 1648, the Iroquois attacked St. Joseph Mission in Teanaustaye, where Father Daniel was serving. He tried to baptize as many of his catechumens as he could and then urged the Hurons to flee. Afterwards he went out to meet the Iroquois. Arrows immediately hit him, his body was thrown into his chapel, and the chapel set on fire.

On March 16, 1649, the Iroquois attacked the Huron village

where Fathers de Brébeuf and Lalemant were stationed. The priests were taken captive, stripped and beaten all over their bodies. The Indians cut off their hands, applied red-hot hatchets to their bodies, and poured boiling water on them. As Father de Brébeuf continued to preach to them, the Indians gagged him, cut off his nose and tore off his lips. Then they slashed pieces of flesh from the priests' bodies, roasted them, and ate them. Finally, they killed them by cutting an opening above their breasts and tearing out their hearts, which they also ate.

Father Garnier was the next to be martyred. The Iroquois attacked an unprotected village where he was serving, killing the Huron women, children and aged. Father Garnier hurried from place to place, giving absolution to as many Christians as he could and baptizing children and catechumens. He was hit by two bullets from a musket fired by one of the Indians and then a tomahawk blow ended his life.

Father Chabanel, Father Garnier's assistant, was absent when the village was attacked. Returning to the village, he and his companions could hear the cries of the Hurons as they were being massacred. Father Chabanel urged his Indian companions to flee and he, too, tried to follow them. For a long time it wasn't known whether he had managed to make his escape, but it was finally determined that he was killed, not by an Iroquois but by an apostate Huron who hated the Christian faith.

By the end of the Iroquois attacks of 1648 and 1649, there was not much left of the fifteen Huron villages. The missionaries who were not martyred led the survivors to safety near French settlements. Later Huron villages were established in what is now northern Michigan.

Pope Pius XI beatified the eight martyrs—Isaac Jogues, René Goupil and John de Lalande, killed in the United States, and John de Brébeuf, Anthony Daniel, Gabriel Lalemant, Charles Garnier and Noel Chabanel, killed in Canada—in 1925 and canonized them in 1930. Their feast is observed on October 19.

CHAPTER 5

Blessed Kateri Tekakwitha

(1656-1680)

Ten years after the Mohawk Indians martyred Isaac Jogues and John de Lalande in the village of Ossernenon, near modern Auriesville, New York, a baby girl was born there in 1656. She was the daughter of a Mohawk chief named Kenhoronkwa, the war chief of the village and of the Tortoise clan. She was given the name Tekakwitha. Her mother, Kahenta, was an Algonquin Indian woman who had been captured during a raid by the Mohawks on her village.

Kahenta was a Christian when she was captured, but was never again allowed to practice her religion. She was a gentle and kind woman, though, and as she carried her daughter about on her back as she worked, she undoubtedly sang the hymns she had learned back in Quebec. Kahenta was an influence on her young daughter.

When Tekakwitha was only four years old, a smallpox epidemic broke out in the village. Kenhoronkwa, Kahenta and their small son all died of the disease, and Tekakwitha caught it, too. Eventually, the disease ran its course and Tekakwitha survived. However, the illness left her severely pockmarked and half blind. For the rest of her life, she saw only shadows, and sunshine hurt her eyes.

With the death of their war chief, the women elders elected his successor. They chose Iowerano, Kenhoronkwa's brother. He, his wife, and an aunt moved into the chief's longhouse and the care of Tekakwitha was given to them. The women elders also decided that Ossernenon held too many bad memories because of all the deaths that occurred there. All the surviving residents moved their village to Auries' Creek and began a new village called Gandawague.

As Tekakwitha grew up, she lived a normal Indian child's life in the love of her new family. She was given domestic chores, such as pounding corn to make flour, and she became adept at embroidering headbands, leggings, and belts. But she was withdrawn from other children, perhaps because of her poor eyesight. From the time of her childhood, she enjoyed the solitude that the wilderness provided. She was well on her way to becoming the mystic she was to be within a few years.

As she matured, the women in the village, as was common among the Iroquois and Mohawk Indians, began making plans for her marriage. As the chief's daughter, and known for her gentle nature and industriousness, she was considered a potentially good wife, despite her physical disfigurement and poor eyesight. But Tekakwitha adamantly refused to even discuss marriage and she rejected a very eligible young man her aunts invited to their longhouse.

This was strange behavior indeed for a Mohawk woman. Remaining unmarried was unheard of and her refusal of the youth selected for her earned the enmity of the women elders of the village. From then on Tekakwitha received harsh treatment from the women, who laughed at her, mocked her, and made sure she had the most demeaning chores. She was no longer the beloved daughter, but was reduced to the status of a slave.

Since the murder of the eight Jesuit martyrs in 1646 and 1649, and the defeat of the Hurons, allies of the French, by the Iroquois, missionaries had stayed away from Iroquois, and particularly Mohawk, territory. But the Mohawk chiefs approved a peace treaty in 1667, and three Jesuit priests—Jacques Fremin, Jean Pierron and Jacques Bruyas—decided to make another attempt to convert the Indians, accepting whatever might lay in wait for them.

Because of the peace treaty, the missionaries were greeted with ceremony when they arrived. Tekakwitha's uncle even put his longhouse at their disposal. Tekakwitha didn't say much to them, but did ask how long they planned to stay. This was not just an idle question, although the missionaries considered it such. For some time she felt that something was missing in her life and she was happy to see the Blackrobes she had heard about.

The missionaries began five missions in Mohawk territory, including a chapel in Gandawague. Father Pierron was stationed there. He worked tirelessly among the Indians and succeeded in making some converts. The Jesuits were cautious about administering baptism, though, because they knew from experience that sometimes the Indians apostatized, and apostate Indians often proved to be the most vicious enemies of the priests. The priests did, though, try to change the lifestyle of the Indians, especially the sexual promiscuousness they found among the youth.

Tekakwitha's uncle distrusted the missionaries. He had seen that many of the Indians who became Christians abandoned their villages and moved to the Mission of Saint Francis Xavier at La Prairie on the Saint Lawrence River. Later the mission was moved to Sault Saint Louis and became known as the Sault Mission ("Sault" means rapids).

In 1670, Father Francis Boniface replaced Father Pierron. Father Boniface could speak the Mohawk language and he translated Christian hymns, prayers and the catechism. At Christmas time, he built a creche in Iroquois design and structure. However, Tekakwitha remained uninvolved, taking everything in but keeping to herself.

An Indian named Kryn, a Mohawk chief who had converted to Christianity, appeared at the village and told the Indians about the Sault Mission, which he described as a paradise of love and faith where the Indians lived in harmony and service to the Christian God. As Iowerano had feared, in 1673 some forty Mohawks left Gandawague and moved to Sault Mission. Father Boniface led them there and then returned to the village, but he suddenly died there in December of 1674.

Father Jacques de Lamberville was sent as Father Boniface's replacement. One day, as he passed Tekakwitha's longhouse, he felt compelled to go in. Tekakwitha had hurt her foot and was there with two other Indian maidens. Tekakwitha welcomed Father de Lamberville and began to tell him about her Christian mother and about the knowledge of the Catholic faith that she had been able to pick up. She told him about the prayers she was saying privately and then said that she wanted to become a Christian.

Father de Lamberville began to give Tekakwitha instructions with his other catechumens. She arrived at the mission regularly, not only to study, but also to attend the church services, which she grew to love. The priest went about the village making inquiries about her character and found that she had an excellent reputation. Surprisingly, neither her uncle nor any other member of her family objected to her conversion.

Tekakwitha was baptized on Easter Sunday of 1676 and given the Christian name Catherine, or Kateri, in honor of Saint Catherine of Siena. She was twenty years old.

As Kateri learned more about her namesake, a true mystic and contemplative, she began to emulate her. She spent long hours in prayer, became particularly attached to the rosary, and began some of the severe penances that some mystics have inflicted upon themselves. She learned to live always in the presence of God. She became, as she has been known ever since, the Lily of the Mohawks and the Mystic of the Wilderness.

But the act of withdrawing from her community, as she did, served only to antagonize other Mohawks, especially other Indian women her age. They again began to mock her and to shout cruel insults at her, as they had done when she refused to marry. When she began to refrain from work on Sundays and holy days, even though she worked extra hard before and afterward, her family responded by forbidding her to eat that day. As the persecution continued, Father de Lamberville became more and more concerned about her welfare. He prayed for a solution.

His prayers were answered in the form of an Oneida chief named Okenratariken, known to the French as Hot Cinders because of his fiery temper. He had been known as a fierce warrior prior to his conversion to Christianity. After that, his personality changed drastically. He administered Indian affairs at Sault Mission and went on journeys throughout the Iroquois territories. In 1677, Hot Cinders arrived in Gandawague accompanied by a Huron Indian and a male relative of Kateri's mother.

Kateri's uncle was not in the village at the time, and Father de Lamberville persuaded Hot Cinders to take Kateri with them to the Sault Mission. Kateri was enthusiastic about going because of all she had heard from Hot Cinders and Kryn about this mission. Hot Cinders, Kateri, the relative and the Huron Indian went to their canoes. Hot Cinders, however, did not accompany the others. He paddled off in the opposite direction to visit his own people in Oneida territory. The Huron Indian was in his own canoe and Kateri was in a canoe with her relative.

Soon after the four left, a cry went up in the village that Kateri had been taken away and a runner was sent to find her uncle. Angry at what he thought was a kidnaping, Iowerano hurried back to his village, got his gun, and began to paddle furiously in pursuit. Not recognizing the Huron, who had doubled back in order to go to a French village for food, he passed him by. The Huron, though, apparently knew Iowerano and he fired a shot in the air to warn Kateri and her relative. They abandoned their canoe and raced through the forest trails to try to get away.

Iowerano saw the canoe and he, too, ran through the forest. At one point, he came upon an Indian sitting next to the trail smoking, but he paid him no attention and continued on the way. The Indian was Kateri's mother's relative, but Iowerano didn't know him. Kateri was carefully hidden among the trees. Iowerano searched for several hours and finally gave up. Kateri and the relative then were able to continue their journey, in effect retracing the steps of her Christian mother decades before. They arrived at the Sault Mission with a letter from Father de Lamberville to the priests there in which he told them: "I send you a treasure, guard it well."

Saint Francis Xavier of Sault Saint Louis was built entirely for the Indian converts. It consisted of a chapel and adjoining work areas and residences for the priests, with sixty cabins for the Christian Indians located outside the mission. The Indian population numbered about 120 to 150. The Indians lived there much as they did in their home villages but they had all the services of the Catholic Church easily available to them.

Kateri was ecstatically happy there. Not only was she able to deepen her piety without fear of persecution, but she met relatives of her mother. It was decided that she should live with the relative who brought her to the mission, and his wife. Another woman who shared the residence was named Anastasia, who had been a close friend of Kateri's mother before her capture by the Mohawks.

Kateri began her day with Mass at dawn and then usually remained in prayer until the second Mass at 8 a.m. She prayed throughout the day, especially with the Brotherhood of the Holy Family at 1 p.m. and with the whole congregation that joined in Vespers at 3 p.m. That service usually ended with Benediction.

She also intensified her penances, physical punishments she inflicted upon herself in reparation for her sins (although they must have been slight indeed) and those of the Mohawk people. She used switches to beat her back and shoulders, walked barefoot in the snow, sometimes stayed awake throughout the night in prayer, and limited herself to one bowl of porridge a day. These practices are similar to those that Saint Rose of Lima, as well as numerous other saints, performed. Later she even increased her suffering, branding herself with faggots, wearing an iron chain around her waist, and trying to sleep on thorns.

Although she tried to remain hidden, her reputation for sanctity grew. The priests decided that it was time for her to make her First Communion. Catholics did not receive Holy Communion as frequently then as they do now and not as early in their childhood. So Kateri made her First Communion on Christmas Day, 1677.

In 1678, Kateri discovered another aspect of the spiritual life. She visited Ville Marie, the city of Montreal, and there discovered women who belonged to religious orders. Of course, there was never a thought then that an Indian could join a religious community, but Kateri returned to Sault Mission and spoke to two other women about what she had seen in Ville Marie. They planned to establish a community of their own, wear similar clothes, and follow a routine of prayer and work. But when they presented their idea to the priest, he met the idea with laughter.

Kateri was disappointed and made another trip to Ville Marie to learn more about the vows the women religious there took. After her return, she approached Father Cholonec and asked him to allow her to make a vow of perpetual virginity. He was astonished since the idea of maintaining one's virginity was completely foreign to the Indians. But he agreed to allow her to do so, and on the feast of the Annunciation, March 25, 1679, Kateri consecrated her virginity to Christ.

By early 1680, Kateri's health was failing as a result of her heavy penances. She was no longer able to leave her cabin and was confined to her bed, wracked with pain. Members of the Brotherhood of the Holy Family kept vigil with her as her condition worsened. The priests brought Viaticum to her, unusual in those days when it was not normal to take the Blessed Sacrament out of the chapel. She received Extreme Unction shortly before she died on April 17, 1680, with the names of Jesus and Mary on her lips. She was only 24.

After Kateri died and was laid out on a pallet, the people around her gasped. As they watched, her skin lightened, becoming radiant and white, and the pockmarks on her face disappeared. It was no longer the body of a frail, dark and scarred young woman, but that of a beautiful young maiden. Two Frenchmen, who were well acquainted with Kateri, made an elaborate coffin for her and she was buried beside the river.

After her death she became well known to the Native Americans throughout the United States. Pope John Paul II beatified her on June 22, 1980. Her feast is celebrated on July 14.

Chapter 6

Saint Marguerite Bourgeoys
(1620-1700)

When Kateri Tekakwitha visited Ville Marie, now the city of Montreal, in 1678, and discovered women living there in religious communities, one of those communities was the Congregation de Notre Dame of Montreal. That community was founded by Marguerite Bourgeoys, a true pioneer of French Canada and now an American saint. Sister Bourgeoys served the people of New France for 47 years.

She was born in Troyes, France on Good Friday, April 17, 1620, and baptized the same day. She was the third of twelve children of Abraham and Guillemette Bourgeoys. When Marguerite was seventeen, her mother died after giving birth to another daughter, and Marguerite devoted the next several years to caring for her baby sister.

When she was twenty, she had a life-changing experience as she participated in an outdoor procession in honor of Our Lady of the Rosary. As she passed a statue of the Blessed Virgin, she thought that it came alive and that the Blessed Virgin herself had looked at her. Feeling a vocation to devote her life to the service of God, she tried to enter a Carmelite convent, but was turned down. She fared no better when she applied to enter a convent of Poor Clares.

The French religious communities were flourishing at the time and convents were crowded. Marguerite, therefore, decided to join a group of lay women who served as externs for cloistered nuns in Troyes.

A little later, Marguerite and two friends opened a private school. It didn't last long, though, because one of the friends married and the other died. The school closed.

She was back to working with the externs when she learned from a friend, Sister Louise, that the cloistered sister's brother was looking for a woman willing to go to New France and teach the children there. The nun's brother was Paul de Chomedy de Maisonneuve, the founder and governor of Ville Marie (City of Mary). He and his small group of pioneers had arrived at the foot of Mount Royal and founded Ville Marie on May 18, 1642. The group of pioneers, known as the Company of Ladies and Gentlemen of Ville Marie, had received a charter from the king of France to establish a Catholic settlement in New France.

The new settlement didn't exactly thrive at first. After eleven years only seventeen people lived there. So Maisonneuve returned to France in 1653 in search of new colonists, and it was at that time that he spoke to his sister about the need for a teacher in Ville Marie for the settlers' children. Sister Louise recommended Marguerite and then told Marguerite about the need. Marguerite sought the advice of several priests and then agreed to go to Ville Marie.

Maisonneuve managed to round up 108 men for his little colony. Their expenses were to be paid by the Company of Ladies and Gentlemen of Ville Marie if they agreed to stay for at least five years. Besides the men, who boarded the *Saint Nicholas* on June 20, 1653, there were a half dozen women who were going to Ville Marie as prospective brides, and Marguerite Bourgeoys.

It was a terrible voyage. The old ship began leaking water and it soon became evident that it was not sea worthy. It returned to port and the voyagers had to find another ship. They set sail once again on July 20. Then illness broke out on board and eight men died. Marguerite tended to the sick as well as she could despite having no medical training. They finally reached Quebec on September 22 and were greeted warmly by the people in the fort located there. Among those who greeted them was Jeanne Mance, a woman who had been among the first settlers of Ville Marie in 1642 and who had founded a hospital, the Hotel Dieu. After resting in Quebec for a while, the travelers took another two weeks to complete the journey up the St. Lawrence River to Ville Marie, arriving there in November 1653.

At first, Marguerite lived in the governor's house with Jeanne Mance and the girls who had come to marry settlers. She worked as housekeeper, helped at the hospital, and chaperoned the prospective brides. In later years, as more and more young women came from France, she trained them in housekeeping chores and served as a surrogate mother to them.

She also taught catechism to the few children then living at Ville Marie, but it wasn't until April 30, 1658 that she opened a school for seven children. The school was a former stable, measuring 18 by 26 feet, with the bare ground as its floor and a loft that was reached by an outside ladder. This small building also became Marguerite's home, and she shared it with three Indian children.

Soon the settlement began to thrive and the number of children in the school increased considerably. Marguerite needed help in the school and Jeanne Mance needed more help in the hospital. So in September 1658 the two pioneer women went back to France in search of new recruits. In June 1659 they began the return voyage, each with three women assistants and a Brother Louis, who agreed to teach the boys at Ville Marie. A dozen future brides were also in Marguerite's charge.

Once again Marguerite had a bad experience on the sea voyage. A violent storm almost wrecked the ship, and sickness again broke out among the 200 passengers, killing some of the young women who had hoped to become brides. It was October by the time the travelers reached Ville Marie.

The settlement had now grown to about 400 people. Marguerite added a vocational school to the school she had originally founded. She and the other teachers lived in community and began to observe a rule of life, but did not take any vows. The little school became their convent until a new and larger stone house could be built. Marguerite was now called Sister Bourgeoys.

In 1669, Bishop François de Montmorency Laval of Quebec recognized the group as a religious community under the name Daughters of the Congregation, and he gave them permission to teach wherever they might be asked to go in New France. The sisters adopted a habit that included a black dress, black belt and veil, and a white linen cornette and kerchief.

Marguerite made a second voyage back to France in 1670. This time she was away from her congregation in Ville Marie for almost two years. During that time, among other things, she obtained official approval from the king for her congregation and managed to recruit nine new members.

By 1676 the community consisted of fifteen members and Marguerite asked Bishop Laval to raise the group to the status of a congregation of secular sisters by authorizing them to take simple vows. The bishop did so but postponed giving them a permanent rule until later. It was at this time that the community was given the name Congregation of Notre Dame of Montreal.

The sisters opened a boarding school for girls in 1677 and new day schools were established as new settlements sprang up. When the Sulpician Fathers founded an Indian mission on Mount Royal, Marguerite's sisters taught the children there. In 1678, the first stone church in Montreal was completed.

Marguerite was still anxious to receive official approval of a permanent rule for her community. In 1679, Bishop Laval was in Paris. Marguerite made her third visit there, hoping to get Bishop Laval's approval of a rule. The sisters were now established in five different places in New France, but only Marguerite's leadership was holding them together. This mission was a failure. Not only did Bishop Laval refuse to approve a permanent rule for the congregation, but he also forbade Marguerite to recruit any new sisters in France. She returned to Montreal greatly disappointed.

Tragedy struck the congregation on December 6, 1683 when fire destroyed their new building and two sisters were burned to death. While a new motherhouse was being constructed, the sisters stayed in their old houses and at the Hotel Dieu.

Meanwhile, disagreement with Bishop Laval continued. In 1684 he went to Montreal and tried to convince Marguerite to merge her congregation with the Ursuline Sisters in Quebec. Marguerite, though, was convinced that her sisters should not be bound by strict enclosure, as the Ursulines were, and that they should take only simple vows. Marguerite offered to resign as superior of her community, but that offer was refused.

A year later, Bishop Laval was succeeded by Bishop Jean Baptiste de Saint Vallier. Again Marguerite asked to be relieved of her position as superior, and the new bishop finally consented in 1693, when Marguerite was 73 years old. The sisters elected Sister Marie Barbier and Marguerite was named one of her counselors and "admonisher." She had now been at Ville Marie for forty years, except for the three trips back to France. Her community now numbered forty women and they were established in seven different places in New France.

Marguerite spent the last years of her life in retirement and prayer. She lived long enough to see the congregation she founded receive official episcopal approbation with a permanent rule on June 24, 1698. The sisters made their profession, taking simple vows of poverty, chastity, obedience and commitment to the work of teaching girls. They also each received a religious name. Marguerite selected Sister Marguerite of the Blessed Sacrament.

Marguerite died on January 12, 1700, three months short of her eightieth birthday. The residents along the St. Lawrence River regarded her as a saint and Pope Pius XII beatified her on November 12, 1950. Pope John Paul II canonized her on October 31, 1982. Her feast is celebrated on January 12.

CHAPTER 7

Saint Marie Marguerite D'Youville

(1701-1771)

There are many parallels between the lives of Saint Marie Marguerite d'Youville, the first native-born Canadian to be canonized, and Saint Elizabeth Ann Seton, the first native-born resident of the future United States to be canonized. Both were married and widowed, both experienced the heartache of seeing some of their children die, both had to struggle to care for their children after the deaths of their husbands, both had to endure criticism and opposition, and both were founders of religious communities for women.

Marie Marguerite d'Youville came first. She was born 73 years before Elizabeth Ann Seton and died three years before Elizabeth Ann was born. Marie Marguerite was born on October 15, 1701, in Varennes, near Montreal, only a year and nine months after Saint Marguerite Bourgeoys died in Montreal. She was the eldest of six children, three boys and three girls, of Christophe Dufrost de Lajemmerais and Marie Renée Gaultier de Varennes.

The family lived on a small farm and Marie Marguerite's father barely eked out a living. Then, when Marie Marguerite was only seven, the plight of the family grew worse when Christophe died. Now it was up to her mother and the little children to till the soil and raise the crops on the farm. Marie Marguerite helped as much as a young child could.

When she was eleven, Marie Marguerite was sent to a school in Quebec operated by the Ursuline Sisters because the family had a relative among the nuns. There she absorbed the French spirituality of the Ursulines who taught her to trust in God and to serve those less fortunate. However, she was there for only two years because her mother needed her at home. She was tall and strong for her age, and proved to be a big help to her mother. She helped to teach her younger brothers and sisters.

As Marie Marguerite matured, she had more time to associate with others her age and she soon became popular among the young men and women of Varennes. She fell in love with a young man there and they became engaged, but then her mother remarried an Irish doctor whom Varennes society thought of as a foreigner and beneath her social class. This so offended the family of her fiancé that he broke their engagement.

After her mother's remarriage, the family sold the small farm and moved from Varennes to Montreal. When she was twenty, Marie Marguerite again fell in love and married François d'Youville, who seemed to be a pleasant young man with good connections with the governor-general of New France, and moderately wealthy. The couple moved into the home of François' mother.

Unfortunately, the marriage turned out to be unhappy. Problems with her mother-in-law, who was a domineering woman, began soon after the marriage. Furthermore, François turned out to be a selfish man who cared little about Marie Marguerite's wishes. Unknown to Marie Marguerite prior to the wedding, his wealth came from the illegal sale of alcohol to the Indians and François spent his money on drink. He was absent a good part of the time dealing with the Indians. Marie Marguerite tried to be a good wife. She bore six children, but four of them died young. The two remaining, François and Charles, eventually became priests.

The marriage lasted eight years, until François died of "acute inflammation of the lungs," the result of his dissipated life. When he died, he had not only spent all of his money but he had debts totaling eleven thousand pounds. The man who seemed to have so much promise eight years earlier now had a terrible reputation. Marie Marguerite, at 28, was a destitute widow with heavy debts, two children to support, and another on the way. A year later that child died, too.

She opened a small shop on the first floor of her home where she sold her own handiwork and various household items. Since she had been accustomed to hard work all of her life, she soon began to prosper. Within a few years she managed to pay off her husband's debts and had enough income to pay for a good education for her sons. She also made generous contributions to organizations serving the poor people of Montreal.

But she wanted to do more than make monetary contributions. She became a volunteer at the hospital, helping to care for the sick, cleaning their rooms and mending their clothes. Soon she was spending more and more time at the hospital.

By 1737, Marie Marguerite was a 36-year-old single mother. Her fourteen-year-old son, François, was already studying to be a priest in a Sulpician seminary, and she was living alone with her eight-year-old son, Charles. Her small shop was doing well and she was devoting many hours to helping in the hospital. But she felt dissatisfied and knew that God was calling her to do more. She had long been a member of the Confraternity of the Holy Family and had a Sulpician priest, Father Gabriel Dulescoat, as her spiritual director. She was accustomed to praying, "Lord, make known to me the way I should walk."

She felt convinced that she was being called to devote the rest of her life to the practice of the works of mercy. She discussed the matter with Father Dulescoat, who told her, "God has destined you for a great work." She finally decided to convert her own home into a shelter for the poor and helpless people of Montreal and to provide for their needs. On November 21, 1737, she welcomed a blind woman into her home. This action inspired three other women who felt called to share in her mission. The four women began to live together in Marie Marguerite's home. They opened the home to the poor and began to care for them.

The citizens of Montreal did not take kindly to this new venture. This just wasn't something that was done by respectable women. Furthermore, despite the good work Marie Marguerite had been doing, her late husband's reputation stuck to her. She and her companions became the objects of gossip, people wondering if all the suspicious people who were constantly visiting the home didn't indicate that the women were involved in some kind of illegal activity, perhaps the sale of liquor to the Indians as her husband had done. The women were insulted when they appeared in public. They were given the name *les Soeurs Grises*—"the Tipsy Sisters." For a time the local priest believed the rumors about the women and they were publicly refused Holy Communion because of their dubious reputation.

They had other setbacks, too. Fire destroyed their home. They moved to another home and were immediately evicted from it. One of the women died. But through it all, the women persevered and eventually the people's attitudes changed. After they did, and the women's good reputation was finally restored, the women decided to retain the name *les Soeurs Grises*. The French word *gris* means "grey" as well as "tipsy," and Marie Marguerite, displaying a sense of humor, adopted a grey religious habit for the women. They were now known as the Grey Nuns.

Soon other young women joined Marie Marguerite and her companions. By 1745 the women were formally established as the religious community of the Sisters of Charity and a rule for the community was approved on June 15, 1755.

In 1747, when the community was still operating under a provisional rule, the General Hospital of Montreal was given to the Sisters of Charity. It had a debt of 49,000 French pounds and was in danger of being closed. The entire debt came with the title to the property. It was a risky undertaking, to be sure, but Marie Marguerite was convinced that God would see them through. Besides, she had learned how to pay off debts after her husband died.

She even increased the debt by completely renovating the dilapidated hospital, repairing part of it and completely rebuilding other parts. With a greater capacity, the sisters then opened it to everyone who was sick—the incurable, the insane, aged, lepers, and those suffering from contagious diseases. She also opened a home for foundlings and orphans, the first in North America.

To help pay off the debt, Marie Marguerite herself made clothing that was sold in the local shops to residents and the traders who came to Montreal. Payment for these clothes became one of the main sources of income for the sisters and the hospital.

Always a bundle of energy, Marie Marguerite also bought several farms in the area to support 118 needy people. While the adults were farming, she taught catechism to the children. Later she organized spiritual retreats for the women.

The years 1755 to 1763 marked the so-called French and Indian War, the American counterpart of the Seven Years War between France and England. During the war, the Sisters of Charity increased their work at the hospital, caring for wounded soldiers of both sides. At one point, Marie Marguerite ransomed an English prisoner from the Indians so they couldn't torture him, and they saved a number of soldiers from the Indians. During the siege of Quebec, Father Charles, Marie Marguerite's younger son, was imprisoned aboard an English frigate along with his parishioners. They were released four months later, after the surrender of Quebec.

For the Canadians, the war ended with the conquest of the French by the English at Quebec in 1760. It was a sad time for the Catholic Church in Canada. The Treaty of Paris gave Canada to Great Britain and a period of religious persecution followed, despite the guarantee in the treaty that Canadians could enjoy "the free exercise of their religion, as far as is permissible under the laws of Great Britain." The laws of Great Britain at the time didn't provide much protection for Catholics.

Catastrophe struck the Sisters of Charity in 1766 when the General Hospital in Montreal was destroyed by fire. Marie Marguerite's reaction, as in all that she did, was to accept the calamity as God's will. She and her sisters knelt in the ashes and prayed the *Te Deum*. A new hospital was built despite the heavy debt the sisters incurred.

Mother Marie Marguerite continued her work until she suffered a partial paralysis in 1771. After a short illness, she died on December 23 of that year, at the age of seventy. All the people of Montreal recognized her for her sanctity.

The Sisters of Charity, the Grey Nuns, spread throughout Canada and, later, into the United States. Soon missionary activities took them to Alaska, China, Japan, Africa, New Guinea, South America, the Bahamas, the Dominican Republic, and Haiti. Their primary mission remained hospital work, but they also conducted schools and orphanages. Today Marie Marguerite's followers are members of six autonomous congregations: Sisters of Charity of Montreal ("Grey Nuns"), Sisters of Charity of Saint Hyacinthe, Sisters of Charity of Ottawa, Sisters of Charity of Quebec, Grey Nuns of the Sacred Heart, and Grey Sisters of the Immaculate Conception.

Pope John XXIII beatified Marie Marguerite d'Youville on May 3, 1959 and called her "Mother of Universal Charity." Pope John Paul II canonized her on December 9, 1990. Her feast is celebrated on October 16.

CHAPTER 8

Blessed Junípero Serra

(1713-1784)

While French Catholics were colonizing Canada and the northern areas of what is now the United States, Spanish missionaries were still working among the Indians of Mexico, Central and South America. Then, in the latter half of the eighteenth century, they began to move into what is now the southern part of the United States and up the West Coast into California. The man who led the missionary expeditions into California was a small Franciscan priest named Junípero Serra.

He is recognized not only by the Church but also by the United States government as the "founder of California." The nine missions he founded up the coast, plus the twelve more that were founded by his successors after his death, are now some of the largest and most important cities of the state—San Diego, San Francisco, Santa Clara, Los Angeles. Every state has two statues in Statuary Hall in the U.S. Capitol in Washington, and one of California's is that of Fray Junípero Serra.

Father Serra was in California only the last fifteen years of his life. During those years, he baptized 6,736 Indians and confirmed more than 5,000. He also brought unprecedented prosperity to at least six different linguistic stocks of natives who were gathered into the missions. It has been estimated that he traveled 5,400 miles by sea and 5,525 by land to visit his missions. His own mission was San Carlos Borromeo at Carmel and he would sometimes travel by ship from nearby Monterey Bay to San Diego and then return by land, baptizing, confirming and performing weddings as he went. He would then continue north to the Santa Clara and San Francisco missions.

Serra was born in the village of Petra on the Spanish island of Majorca on November 24, 1713, son of Antonio and Margarita Serra. At his baptism he was given the name Miguel José. When he was sixteen he applied for admission to the Franciscan order. At first he was rejected because he was short and frail-looking. However, other Franciscans convinced the superior to change his mind, and Miguel was admitted.

During his novitiate year, Miguel learned about the missionaries and their work in New Spain. Francis Solano, who had just been canonized in 1726, especially intrigued him. Miguel's reading about the missionaries stirred his desire to follow in their footsteps, but that wouldn't happen for another nineteen years.

He made his profession on September 15, 1731, when he was eighteen, and took the name Junípero for Brother Juniper, who had been Saint Francis's close friend. He spent the next eighteen years at the Convent of San Francisco in Palma, first as a student and then as a professor of philosophy and theology. He was ordained a priest in 1737.

Serra became recognized as a learned teacher and preacher. However, he never lost his desire to be a missionary. When a Franciscan priest arrived at the convent recruiting priests for the perilous work of converting the Indians of northeastern Mexico to Christianity, Serra volunteered. So did Father Francisco Palou, one of his students, who would remain Serra's close friend and, eventually, his first biographer. They were two of 33 recruits, some Franciscans and some Dominicans. They said good-bye to their parents and religious family, left their island home forever and sailed to Mexico. Serra was 35 and Palou was 26.

It was a difficult journey. During a storm in the Caribbean Sea it appeared that the ship would sink, but the ship and those aboard survived. Ninety-nine days after they left Majorca, they reached Vera Cruz, Mexico. From there they still had to walk 250 miles to Mexico City, through tropical forests, over high mountains, and up to an altitude of 7,382 feet. Serra and Palou walked a little more than fifteen miles a day. Somewhere along the way, Serra's left foot became swollen, apparently the result of a mosquito bite. This resulted in an affliction that was to torment him for the rest of his life.

The two reached the College of San Fernando in Mexico City on January 1, 1750. They would be under the jurisdiction of the Franciscans there the rest of their lives.

Serra's first assignment was the remote, untamed Sierra Gorda country in the Sierra Madre mountains. To get there he and the soldiers and Christian Indians who accompanied him had to walk sixteen days through more tropical forests. Once again, his foot began to swell and his infected sores were painful.

Serra worked in Sierra Gorda for more than eight years. He learned the natives' language and gradually got the Indians to trust him and convert to Christianity. He also taught them better methods of agriculture and how to sell their superfluous products.

He was then recalled to the College of San Fernando in Mexico City and from 1758 to 1767 he preached in and around Mexico City. During those nine years he walked an estimated 5,500 miles, despite his ulcerated leg, preaching to Spaniards, Creoles, and Indians.

During all this he was practicing the penances that he would perform for the rest of his life. He usually slept from eight to midnight, prayed the midnight office, and continued his prayers until dawn. His only other sleep was a siesta after lunch. He ate sparingly, mainly fruit, vegetables and fish. To bring his body into subjection, he wore a sackcloth of bristles next to his skin. Also, like others in this book, he regularly whipped himself "for my own imperfections and sins, as well as the sins of others." He even did this while he was preaching. In imitation of Saint Francis Solano, he would drop his habit to his waist and lash himself. These were all practices approved by the religious authorities of the day, although they seem extreme today.

In 1767, King Carlos III decided to banish the Jesuits from Spain and its colonies in America. Civil authorities were commanded to round up all Jesuits in some sixteen Mexican missions and take them as prisoners to the port at Vera Cruz. Franciscans were ordered to replace the Jesuits. Serra was chosen as the president of the missions in Baja (Lower) California. He and other missionaries left Mexico City and, traveling at almost twenty miles a day, reached the west coast in 39 days. There they embarked on a ship that took them 200 miles up the peninsula to Loreto, the center of the former Jesuit missions in Baja California. Serra remained at Loreto for more than a year while his men conducted conversion efforts.

While in Loreto, Serra learned that José de Gálvez, King Carlos' visitor general, wanted to settle Monterey in Alta (Upper) California. Serra immediately offered himself as the first volunteer "to erect the bold standard of the cross in Monterey." The two men corresponded and Gálvez said that he agreed with Serra's concept of establishing missions about a day's journey apart in the unexplored territory.

Although Serra's interest in Upper California was spiritual, King Carlos had political motives. He had learned that Russia intended to establish settlements along the Pacific coast, and he wanted to prevent that, keeping the western part of what is now the United States for Spain.

So Fray Junípero was on the move again, 900 miles from Loreto to San Diego. Don Gaspar de Portola was the leader of the expedition, but he tried to persuade Father Serra not to go along because Portola thought that Serra's infected foot had become can-cerous. Serra let the expedition go ahead. Then he followed with two servants, a sick and aging mule, and little else.

Serra was so crippled when he began his journey that two men had to lift him onto his mule. "Good-bye, Francisco," he said to Father Palou, "until we meet in Monterey." Palou replied softly, "Good-bye, Junípero, until eternity."

Serra kept a detailed diary of his long trip to San Diego. He left on April 1, 1769, traveling from mission to mission on the Baja peninsula, often sleeping in uninhabited country. His diary notes that "my left foot had become very inflamed" and "this inflamma-tion has reached halfway up the leg."

Eventually, though, he caught up with Portola's men and was able to travel with them, at times being carried on a stretcher. Soon after they passed the last of the former Jesuit missions, they spot-ted their first pagan Indian men, and Serra was shocked. He wrote, "Then I saw what I could hardly begin to believe when I read about it or was told about it, namely that they go about entirely naked like Adam in paradise before the fall." Later he noted that he hadn't seen any native women yet, and "desired for the present not to see them" for fear that they, too, would be naked. When he finally did see women, though, he was relieved "when I saw them so decently clothed."

They finally arrived at San Diego on July 1, slightly more than three months after they left Loreto, 900 miles away, and 2,000 miles from Mexico City.

The coast of California had more Indians per square mile than any other area of the United States. About 250,000 of them lived in more than 25 linguistic groups. As Serra was searching for the best place to start his mission in San Diego, he continued to no-tice that all the males were entirely naked but all the women, in-cluding female children and babies, wore clothing.

At first all the Indians seemed friendly and welcomed the Spaniards, so Serra turned his attention to constructing his mission on the site he selected, Presidio Hill. He founded his first mission in Upper California, San Diego de Alcalá, on July 16, 1769. He was then 55 years old.

The Indians didn't remain friendly for long, though. On August 15, with only four soldiers guarding the mission, a group of about twenty Indians attacked. Serra's servant was killed with an arrow through his neck. The blacksmith and a Christian Indian were wounded. The soldiers killed some of the attacking Indians and they retreated.

After that attack, the Indians became more peaceful, and Serra was able to continue to try to fulfill his dream of building fifty missions along the California coast. The second mission, after San Diego, was the one in Carmel named for Saint Charles Borromeo, and it was there that Fray Junípero made his headquarters. The presidio, where the Spanish soldiers were located, was at nearby Monterey, about an hour's walk away.

At first, Serra had the cooperation of the Spanish civil authorities in his vision of building missions. But others who did not share his vision replaced those civil authorities and friction arose. It was difficult for Serra to accept what he considered the interference of the civil authorities in strictly religious matters, but it was an era when the king of Spain was supreme in ecclesiastical as well as civil matters, and the king's representatives had authority to make the final decisions.

In 1772, disagreement over jurisdiction became so great that Serra made the long trip back to Mexico City to confer with the Spanish viceroy, Chevalier Antonio Bucareli. Serra and a twelve-year-old Indian servant went by ship thirteen days to San Blas, Baja California. From there they walked eight days to Guadalajara, through the Sierra Madre Mountains. They arrived so ill that they were administered the sacrament of Extreme Unction. They recovered and continued their journey and finally arrived at the College of San Fernando on February 6, 1773, three months after they left Monterey.

The trip was successful because Bucareli issued a decree that "the government, control, and education of the baptized Indians should belong exclusively to the missionaries." This "Regulation" was the basis for the first legislation in California, a sort of "Bill of Rights" for the Indians. The soldiers were to preserve harmony and cooperate with the missionaries.

From then on, Serra was always busy with the details of mission life: the Indians, the missionaries at each of the missions, the planting of crops, the construction of buildings, the scheduling of ships, and the handling of a vast correspondence.

Things seemed to be going smoothly until October of 1775 when about 600 Indians attacked and burned the mission in San Diego. One of the missionaries, Father Luis Jayme, was killed, shot by more than a dozen arrows and then his face crushed. When word reached Serra in Carmel, he was stunned. Then, in a hoarse voice, he said, "Thanks be to God. Now that the terrain has been watered by blood, the conversion of the San Diego Indians will take place." The mission was rebuilt and the Indians pacified.

Then Viceroy Bucareli died and Father Serra had more difficulties with his successors. For a while, civil authorities forbade Serra to confirm his converts, an order that he ignored because he knew that, since the missions were not part of a diocese, the pope had given him permission to confirm. The confirmation controversy dragged on for about two years, from 1778 to 1780, and it caused Serra great anguish.

Junípero Serra remained active until he was seventy, constantly traveling from mission to mission despite his ulcerated left foot and leg, celebrating Mass, baptizing, confirming, and performing weddings. He died peacefully on August 28, 1784, and was buried in the church at the mission in Carmel.

Pope John Paul II beatified Father Serra on September 25, 1988. His feast is celebrated on July 1.

Serra International, an organization of 21,000 members in 673 clubs in 35 countries, is named in his honor. Serra Clubs promote vocations to the priesthood and religious life, and train lay leadership.

CHAPTER 9

Saint Elizabeth Ann Seton

(1774-1821)

Elizabeth Ann Seton was a wife and a mother. She was also the foundress of the parochial school system and the first religious order in the United States.

The first half of her life gave no indication that Elizabeth would end up doing the things that she did. She was then a Protestant, born August 28, 1774 (two years before the Declaration of Independence and the start of the Revolutionary War) into the wealthy and distinguished New York Bayley family. However, by the time she was thirty she was a widow with five children, living in poverty. When she converted to Catholicism she was ostracized from New York society and had to flee to Baltimore to support her family.

Elizabeth's mother was Catherine Charlton, the daughter of the Episcopalian Rector of St. Andrew's Church, Staten Island. She died when Elizabeth was three years old. Her father was Dr. Richard Bayley, a renowned physician as well as professor of anatomy at King's College in New York, an institution that later developed into Columbia University. Elizabeth was reared by her father as a staunch Episcopalian. As such, she learned the value of prayer, Scripture and a nightly examination of conscience. Dr.

Bayley was known as a great humanitarian and he taught his daughter to love and serve others.

Elizabeth's education was similar to that of other high society girls in New York during the eighteenth century. She learned music, French, literature, sewing, dancing, and the skills necessary for a housewife. She took a particular interest in history and religious literature, taking full advantage of her father's extensive library. She was greatly influenced by *The Imitation of Christ* and, of course, the Bible. She began practices that were more Catholic than Episcopalian—wearing a crucifix, bowing her head at the name of Jesus, praying to her guardian angel.

By her late teens, Elizabeth Bayley was the belle of New York society, widely courted by the city's gentlemen. When she was nineteen, she chose William Magee Seton for her husband, a wealthy merchant six years older than she. He was a well-traveled young man, having done business in France and Spain as well as in Italy, where he had been apprenticed to the Filicchis, a family of bankers and shipbuilders.

Their wedding on January 25, 1794 was one of New York's principal social events of the winter. Then, for the next eleven years, Elizabeth and William Seton were a model of the perfect young wealthy American family of that era. Their five children, three girls and two boys, were born within eight years. She became very close to William's sisters Rebecca, Harriet, and Cecilia, all of whom remained loyal to her in years to come.

One note of sadness during that time was the death of Elizabeth's father. He contracted yellow fever while attending to some Irish immigrants with that disease. Elizabeth rushed to his bedside and he died in her arms.

During all this period, Elizabeth's diary shows a deepening of her spirituality, a spirituality she tried to impart to her children— Anna Maria (later called Annina), William, Richard, Catherine (sometimes called Josephine or Kit) and Rebecca. She faithfully attended services at Trinity Episcopal Church where she came under the influence of Rev. Henry Hobart. Unfortunately, he was bitterly anti-Catholic.

This happy family life took an abrupt change in 1803 when Elizabeth was 29. Her husband's health and business both began to fail. William Seton, suffering from blood in his lungs and dysentery, was advised by his doctor to sail to Italy to visit the Filicchis, hoping that his health would improve in Italy. Elizabeth knew that she had to accompany William because someone had to care for him. By this time their wealth had dwindled to such an extent that they could take only one child with them, their oldest daughter Anna Maria. The other four children were left with Rebecca, her sister-in-law.

The passage was not a pleasant one. It took 56 days to get to Italy, with William's health continuing to deteriorate and with Anna Maria contracting whooping cough. Elizabeth, of course, had to nurse them both. When they arrived at Italy, jubilant at the thought of getting off the ship, they learned that they could not enter Italy immediately. There had been another attack of yellow fever in New York and their ship didn't have a bill of health to show that its passengers were free of the disease. So the Setons were quarantined in a "pesthouse" on the shore, called a Lazaretto. William had to be carried there and little Anna Maria trembled with fright. A guard was posted to keep the family in the Lazaretto. It was a prison.

The little family was forced to live there from November 19 to December 19, 1803. William's health continued to decline. On December 19, he was carried out of the pesthouse and taken by coach to a house in Pisa. It had been 96 days since they left their home in New York. William lived only eight more days. With the name of Jesus on his lips, he died in Elizabeth's arms. The scene was almost identical to that of the death of Elizabeth's father.

Elizabeth was now a widow. She moved into the home of the Filicchis in Italy until she could return to New York. The Filicchi brothers, Fillipo and Antonio, were devout Catholics as well as successful businessmen. Antonio and his wife Amabilia were to become Elizabeth's closest friends and supporters.

Elizabeth felt spiritually at home with this family that began each day with Mass and where devotion to the Blessed Mother included the daily saying of the rosary. Elizabeth was particularly excited by three basic points of Catholicism: belief in the real presence of Jesus in the Blessed Sacrament, devotion to Mary the Mother of God, and conviction that the Catholic Church could be traced back to Christ and his apostles.

Elizabeth and Anna Maria tried to return to New York in February. However, a severe storm drove the ship back. Furthermore, Anna Maria came down with a high fever and a doctor told Elizabeth that Anna Maria could not survive the journey. The Setons returned again to the Filicchi mansion. Then Elizabeth caught Anna Maria's illness and it seemed for a while that she would not recover. But she did eventually and she and Anna Maria were ready again to sail back to New York to rejoin Elizabeth's other four children. Antonio and Amabilia decided that Antonio should accompany them to New York. He had business to attend to there anyway.

So there was another two-month journey on the Atlantic Ocean before Elizabeth was reunited with her other four children. It was a trip during which she learned much more about the Catholic faith from Antonio, who had prepared a syllabus of Catholic teachings for her.

Shortly after her return to New York, Elizabeth was again at the bedside while a dear one died. This time it was her sister-in-law Rebecca, the confidante of all her diary entries from the time of her departure to Italy until her return.

The next few years were very hard for Elizabeth. Some of her problems were financial. She knew, but William did not when he died, that the family fortune was gone. William had left a will disposing of many possessions that he no longer owned and Elizabeth had obeyed William's doctors who thought it best that he not know that he had lost his wealth. Now Elizabeth had to support herself and her five children.

At the same time, she struggled with her decision about whether to remain an Episcopalian or to become a Catholic. She was torn between following her beliefs and the admonitions of her friends that she not abandon the faith of her family. Dr. Henry Hobart, who had long been a friend and adviser, tried every way possible to keep her an Episcopalian. But she finally made up her mind to become a Catholic and was formally received into the Catholic Church on March 14, 1805. She was thirty years old.

It's hard today to imagine what this decision did to Elizabeth in the eyes of New York society. She was immediately forsaken by most of her family and friends, with the notable exceptions of her two surviving sisters-in-law Cecilia and Harriet Seton, and Julia Scott of Philadelphia. Elizabeth's children, on the other hand, were very happy because they were well aware that making this hard decision had damaged her health. On the day of her First Communion, Elizabeth wrote to Amabilia Filicchi, "My health is pitiful."

But with five children to support, she had to find a job. She had humbly accepted financial help from the Filicchis but knew that her family was her responsibility. First she was invited by an Englishman named White to help him open a school in New York. The school lasted only three months before it had to be closed.

Then an incident happened that convinced Elizabeth that she had to get out of New York. Cecilia Seton, her sister-in-law, became seriously sick and Elizabeth went to care for her. During her convalescence, Cecilia confided that she wanted to become a Catholic like Elizabeth. When Cecilia told her family, they were outraged and blamed Elizabeth. They locked Cecilia in her room and demanded that she break off all relations with the "corrupter of her mind." They even threatened to deport her to the West Indies. But Cecilia finally prevailed and became a Catholic.

The chance for Elizabeth to get out of New York finally came when Father William Du Bourg, the president of St. Mary's Seminary in Baltimore, invited her to open a school for girls in Baltimore. The school opened in June of 1808. It was the first parochial school in the United States. Elizabeth and her children lived in a house on Paca Street with Father Du Bourg's mother and sister.

That summer a priest at St. Mary's Seminary in Baltimore, who had been acting as chaplain for Elizabeth's school, met a girl in Philadelphia, Cecilia O'Conway, who expressed interest in becoming a nun. He told her about Elizabeth Seton and the school, and soon Cecilia came to Baltimore. Shortly afterward, Samuel Sutherland Cooper, a wealthy man who decided to become a priest, donated some of his property in Emmitsburg, 50 miles west of Baltimore, to Elizabeth. Almost without her planning, the nucleus of a religious community was developing.

Soon there were five women aspiring to become nuns. In the spring of 1809, after conferences with Bishop John Carroll, the first bishop of the United States, they formally formed a religious community, calling themselves the Sisters of St. Joseph. Elizabeth was elected their superior and from then on was known as Mother Seton. The community moved to the property in Emmitsburg where, despite extreme hardships for a number of years, the order continued to expand. It also, upon the advice of Bishop Carroll, eventually adopted the rule of an existing community. The sisters chose the Daughters of Charity of St. Vincent de Paul and the order was known from then on as the Sisters of Charity of St. Joseph.

Two of the women who followed Mother Seton were her two surviving sisters-in-law, Cecilia and Harriet. Both were in frail health, though, and both ended up dying in Elizabeth's arms, just as their sister Rebecca and their brother William had done.

Mother Seton continued to lead her community for another twelve years. It spread rapidly. Before her death there were twenty Daughters of Charity communities spread across the United States. The sisters established orphanages and hospitals, but were most renowned for their commitment to the spread of the parochial school system. Today the Daughters of Charity serve and staff hospitals, colleges, high schools and elementary schools, clinics, services for the elderly, and numerous other charities.

Mother Seton also somehow found time to work personally with the poor and the sick, to compose music, write hymns and prepare spiritual discourses. She also continued to care for her children. Her oldest child, Anna Maria, became a postulant in the Emmitsburg community. But her health was never very good, and she died on March 12, 1812, with Elizabeth and Anna Maria's sisters, Catherine and Rebecca, at her bedside. Elizabeth had previously helped her father, her husband, and three sisters-in-law enter eternity. This time it was one of her children.

And it was not the last. Little Rebecca, the youngest child, fell on the ice while ice skating one winter day. She cracked her spine and was unable to walk again. She was put under the care of the best surgeons in the United States at that time, but her health continued to decline. She died in 1815 when she was only fourteen.

Catherine, or Kit, was the second of Elizabeth's two daughters. She too became a nun—not, however, in her mother's community. She eventually became Mother Catherine Seton of the Sisters of Mercy, working with the poor and with prisoners in New York. She died at age 91.

The two Seton boys were sent to Georgetown College, with their tuition and expenses paid for by Antonio Filicchi. The younger boy, Richard, left Georgetown to try to learn banking from the Filicchis. That didn't work out and very little is known about Richard after that. One biographer says that Mother Seton suffered "the heartache of a wayward son." However, we know that he died at age 26 from a disease he contracted while nursing a sick priest.

Elizabeth's oldest son, William, became a midshipman in the U.S. Navy. His mother continued to send letters to him, constantly encouraging him in his faith. But the letters reached him only sporadically. Mother and son did not see each other during the last four years of Mother Seton's life. Finally, William had a chance to visit Emmitsburg and biographers describe an emotional scene of his running to the convent only to learn that Elizabeth had died six months before. William went to the small cemetery where he found the graves of his mother, two sisters and two aunts.

Mother Elizabeth Ann Seton was only 46 when she died on January 4, 1821, with her whole community of sisters around her. Her last word was "Jesus." Pope John XXIII beatified her on March 17, 1963 and Pope Paul VI canonized her on September 14, 1975. Her feast day is celebrated on January 4.

CHAPTER 10

Blessed Marie-Rose Durocher
(1811-1849)

Three foundresses of religious orders for women, now listed among the saints and blesseds of North America, died within seven years of one another, between 1849 and 1856. This chapter and the next two are about them: Blessed Marie-Rose Durocher, Saint Rose Philippine Duchesne, and Blessed Theodore Guérin.

Of the three, Marie-Rose Durocher was the youngest since she died on her 38th birthday. She is also the only one of the three to be born in North America; the other two were born in France.

She was born on October 6, 1811 in a little village near Montreal, Canada called Antoine-sur-Richelieu, the tenth of eleven children of Olivier and Geneviève Durocher. She was given the name Melanie Eulalie when she was baptized on the day of her birth, and called Eulalie. She was reared as the youngest child when her younger sister died nine months after her birth. Her parents were farmers.

She grew up as a mischievous tomboy, according to her father. "Her clothes were always torn, always awry," he once said. "She was full of fun to the extent that her mother was distressed and sometimes said: 'What in the world will we ever do with Eulalie when she grows up?' " However, sickness afflicted her from her earliest days and left her in what was described as "an habitual state of weakness."

Religious practices were part of the family's daily routine and Eulalie grew up with a love for Jesus. When she was ten, her mother decided to send her to boarding school, mainly because she thought she was too frail to walk to church or to school. She registered at the Convent of the Congregation of Notre Dame in Saint Denis across the Richelieu River. She spent two years there, during which time she made her First Communion and received the sacrament of Confirmation, both on the same day.

She returned home when she was twelve and spent the next four years helping her mother run their household, to the extent that her weak health permitted. She learned to make her own clothes, to cook, to clean the house, and to perform all other domestic duties.

During this time, her older sister Seraphine was away at boarding school and, while there, decided to enter religious life. Eulalie, too, was feeling the call to religious life and, when Seraphine left the boarding school, she asked her father to allow her to replace her sister. Her father agreed and Eulalie entered a boarding school in Montreal.

She wasn't there long, though, because of her weak health. Several times she was forced to return home when sickness interrupted her studies. In the space of two years she was probably at the boarding school a total of only six or seven months.

Her parents gave Eulalie a horse, named Caesar, when she was eighteen. She soon became skillful in riding and controlling the horse and the exercise she got from riding improved her health. She rode Caesar to visit friends as well as to Mass in the morning and she returned to the church in the afternoon for visits to the Blessed Sacrament and to Mary's altar. Soon she had more vitality than she had ever had in her life.

Then, when Eulalie was still eighteen, her mother died after a two-week illness. Since she had been so close to her mother, Eulalie was crushed, but she also knew that she must now manage the home for her father and brothers as her mother had done. But she was not to do that for long.

Her brother Theophile had been ordained a priest in 1828 and assigned as assistant pastor at Saint Benôit des Deux Montagnes. When the pastor died, Theophile was appointed pastor. At first he invited the late pastor's niece, who had been living in her uncle's rectory, to remain, but soon realized that the invitation created a delicate situation—a young unmarried woman and a young priest living in the same house. So he asked his father to send Eulalie to direct his household while their oldest sister, Geneviève, and her husband went to live with their father. Eulalie, thinking it was God's will for her, reluctantly agreed.

It proved to be difficult for her because it required her to live in a somewhat higher lifestyle in society than that to which she was accustomed. But she performed her duties calmly and peacefully and was admired by all who came to know her. In the summer of 1831, though, Father Durocher was transferred to Beloeil and Eulalie returned to live with her father.

Within a couple months, Father Durocher was pressuring both Eulalie and their father to come to live with him. They did so in the fall of 1831, when Eulalie was twenty years old, and she served as her brother's housekeeper for the next thirteen years.

The first two years were particularly difficult. The servants in the rectory resented her because they thought she had supplanted them, and they took it out on her by treating her rudely. Eulalie put up with the ill treatment and tried to win their approval with attention and kindnesses.

Her brother didn't help the situation. A man of imposing stature who expected everything to be perfect, he unknowingly kept Eulalie in constant fear that she was not carrying out her duties to his satisfaction. Finally their father recognized what was happening and explained the matter to his son, who immediately took steps to reassure Eulalie of his complete satisfaction. Also, at the suggestion of an observant parishioner, Father Durocher found a companion for Eulalie, a young woman named Melodie Dufresne. The two women soon became inseparable friends.

Father Durocher was known as an outstanding host, and visiting priests usually kept the eight guest bedrooms occupied. During the day the guests seldom saw Eulalie because back stairs led to her and Melodie's apartments. At night, though, Father Durocher insisted that Eulalie occupy the hostess's place. Her manners, courtesy, and natural goodness impressed those who dined with them. Dinners were often long and protracted as the priests discussed the affairs of the Church in general, and the problems of the local diocese in particular. Soon Eulalie became well aware of the needs and difficulties of the Church in Montreal. Among the most obvious needs was better catechesis for the youth of the parish and the archdiocese.

Among the priest guests at the rectory were some who were ill or convalescing from an illness, so Eulalie served as a nurse in addition to her housekeeping duties. She also took an active role in the parish and helped with religion classes. She organized an annual retreat for the young ladies in the parish and at other times planned special workshops for them. She became so well known in the city for her graciousness, spirituality, and leadership that she was called "the saint of Beloeil."

When Eulalie was 29, Bishop Ignace Bourget became Bishop of Montreal. Recognizing the laxity with which the Catholics of the diocese practiced their faith, a shortage of priests, and the need for religious education, he scoured Europe in search of priests and sisters. He was eventually to found four religious communities.

One of the communities he brought to Canada was the Missionary Oblates of Mary Immaculate. Among the priests who came from France was Father Pierre Adrien Telmon, a dedicated priest who was to become Eulalie's spiritual director. The two worked together to form the first parish sodality for women in Canada, called the Congregation of the Daughters of Mary Immaculate. By 1843 sodalities had been established in eleven parishes and six years later they were in another forty parishes. Sodalities for women spread to the United States and were prevalent throughout North America until after the Second Vatican Council. They aimed at preserving young women from worldly dangers and forming them in virtue.

Then Eulalie turned her attention to the religious education of young women, the future mothers who would found Christian homes. She dreamed of having a religious community of women in each parish and she asked Father Telmon to try to get the Sisters of the Holy Names of Jesus and Mary, established in France, to come to Canada. Father Telmon liked the idea and so did a friend of his, Father Louis Moise Brassard, pastor of a church in Longueuil. He convinced the Longueuil parish council to buy a house and land for the sisters.

The sisters in France, though, had no wish to go to Canada. Father Telmon, therefore, encouraged Eulalie and her friend Melodie to found a community. This idea took Eulalie by surprise. No Canadian woman had ever done such a thing, she said, and besides, her brother and her father needed her. When she mentioned the idea to her brother, he said he would oppose it with all his power. He then began to treat her harshly, no longer made her the lady of the house, and even forbade her to receive Communion except on Sundays.

However, Bishop Bourget wanted the establishment in Longueuil and he personally asked Eulalie to dedicate herself to the project. His support encouraged Eulalie and on October 31, 1843, with her two companions, Melodie Dufresne and Henriette Cere, she established the first house of the Congregation of the Sisters of the Holy Names of Jesus and Mary in Longueuil. She was 32 years old. The name of the congregation, their habit, and the Constitutions came from the community in France with the same name. (That community later ceased to exist because of political troubles in France.)

The three foundresses, plus a sister of Henriette Cere who joined the community, moved into the house that the Longueuil parish had bought for them. Besides the four sisters, there were thirteen resident students awaiting them plus some forty day students. Soon new recruits began to arrive and the three foundresses, still postulants, formed the Council. They had no mother superior so they kept an empty chair in the place of honor in their meetings for Mary, the mother of God. Eulalie, however, functioned as superior.

The first highlight of the new order was the clothing ceremony on February 28, 1844, when the postulants became novices. Bishop Bourget presided at the ceremony. It was at this time that they were given their new names: Eulalie was named Sister Marie-Rose, Marie Dufresne became Sister Marie-Agnes, and Henriette Cere was called Sister Marie-Madeleine.

The sisters moved into a new convent in August of 1844 and began a new school year in September with 33 resident students and eighty day students.

On December 8, 1844, the feast of the Immaculate Conception, the three novices made their first profession of vows and Bishop Bourget canonically erected the new congregation. The bishop also formally appointed Sister Marie-Rose superior.

Mother Marie-Rose was to live with her community for only six more years. They were years of great trials that included poverty and misunderstandings, both within the congregation and outside. As the community grew, the sisters moved to the former Hotel Roussel. By 1849 there were 44 sisters teaching 448 pupils.

Mother Marie-Rose's last illness began while she was on a trip to Beloeil during the winter of 1849. She returned with a hacking cough that weakened her day by day. She continued her duties, though, through the spring and summer. She died peacefully before dawn on October 6, 1849, her 38th birthday.

Today the Sisters of the Holy Names of Jesus and Mary continue the teaching mission of their foundress but have expanded their apostolate to include pastoral work, adult education and various ministries to the poor and disadvantaged in Canada, the United States, South Africa, Brazil, Peru and Haiti.

Pope John Paul II beatified Marie-Rose Durocher on May 23, 1982. Her feast is celebrated on October 6.

CHAPTER 11

Saint Rose Philippine Duchesne
(1769-1852)

As a young girl in France, Rose Philippine Duchesne dreamed about life among the Indians in the United States. A Jesuit priest who had worked in Louisiana kindled the dream. It was a dream, however, that didn't come true until she was 72 years old. Well before that, though, she had displayed a strong and dauntless will, both in France during the French Revolution and in Missouri, that became the mark of her holiness.

Rose Philippine was born on August 29, 1769 in Grenoble, the capital of the province of Dauphine in southern France. She was the second of eight children, seven girls and one boy, of Pierre-François and Rose Euphrosine Perier Duchesne. Her older sister died when Philippine was nine. The family lived on the third floor of the large Perier house of her mother's parents. Pierre-François was a distinguished lawyer who was involved in the turbulent politics of eighteenth-century France. He also adopted some of the views of French philosophy that rejected religion in general and Catholicism in particular. Euphrosine, however, was a staunch Catholic and a deeply religious woman who reared her children to be faithful Catholics.

The Duchesne children received most of their education by

tutors in their home, but when Philippine was twelve she and her sister Josephine were sent to board in the Visitation convent at Grenoble. The two girls made their First Communions on Pentecost Sunday, May 19, 1782, and it was at that time that Philippine made up her mind to become a Visitation nun and a missionary to the Indians in America.

However, this was not what her parents, especially her father, had in mind for her. When they learned that Philippine was thinking of becoming a nun, they took her out of the school and let her complete her studies at home. By this time, Philippine's maternal grandparents had died and the Duchesne family occupied the entire Perier residence.

When Philippine was nineteen, her parents decided that it was time for her to marry and they selected a suitable young man for her. Philippine confided to an aunt that she didn't want to marry and that she still wanted to be a nun. The two of them went to the Visitation convent and Philippine asked if she could stay. The superior allowed her to do so and, when her parents came for her, they could not talk her into returning home. She was allowed to remain. However, a year later, when she was ready to take her first vows, her father objected so strongly that she remained a novice for more than four years.

In the 1790's, the French Revolution was in full swing. The Catholic Church had long been linked to the monarchy and the privileged classes, and became one of the targets of the revolutionaries. King Louis XVI went to the guillotine on January 21, 1793 and Maximilien Robespierre's Reign of Terror began. Included in the persecution of the Catholic Church was the suppression of religious orders, so the Visitation convent was closed and Philippine had to return to her family. In Grenoble itself, two priests were guillotined and others were imprisoned in the former Visitation convent, but there were not the atrocities that were committed in Paris, Lyons, Bordeaux and other cities.

During the Reign of Terror, Philippine organized an association of Ladies of Mercy to work with the poor and the sick. She also risked her life to help priests who were in hiding, directing fugitive priests to a country home that her father had purchased in the nearby town of Grane. After Robespierre's fall in 1794, the Ladies of Mercy continued their charitable work, working particularly with the sick. When her mother became ill, though, she returned to the country home in Grane to nurse her and was present at her death on June 30, 1797.

The Concordat of 1801 made it possible for convents to reopen. Philippine personally rented her old convent, now a shambles, and tried to bring back the Visitation nuns. However, the only ones who were persuaded to return were old and unable to endure the harsh conditions that reviving the convent required. Finally, there were only two sisters left.

In 1804 Philippine was introduced to Mother Madeleine-Sophie Barat, who had founded the Society of the Sacred Heart. Mother Barat was ten years younger than Philippine. The two women joined forces, Mother Barat taking over the convent and Philippine becoming a member of the Society of the Sacred Heart. She began her novitiate and made her profession of vows in 1805.

She continued her work among the poor and the sick in France, but did not lose her desire to become a missionary in America. Then in 1817, Bishop William Du Bourg, Bishop of Louisiana, visited Mother Barat and asked her to send nuns to his diocese. After Mother Barat agreed, Philippine was the first to volunteer. Mother Barat chose five nuns to go to Louisiana with Philippine as their superior. She would now be known as Mother Duchesne.

The five nuns started their journey in March 1818, when Philippine was 49. Like most trans-Atlantic voyages in those days, this one was hazardous. The ship and its passengers experienced storms and calms, and even sighted an Argentine pirate ship, but it didn't bother them. It took eleven weeks to reach New Orleans, which they did on May 29, 1818. They stayed there with the

Ursuline Sisters for six weeks until they could continue their journey on a riverboat up the Mississippi River to St. Louis. That part of the journey took another seven weeks.

At St. Louis, the sisters were guests of General Bernard Pratte and his wife. Mother Philippine expected to work in St. Louis, but Bishop Du Bourg had other plans. He wanted them to start their first foundation in St. Charles, Missouri, a place Philippine described as "the remotest village in the United States." There they found a temporary home in the seven-room house of a Mrs. Duquette.

Going to St. Charles was a mistake. Although Mother Duchesne opened a small boarding school and a day school there, the first free school for girls west of the Mississippi, cold and hunger drove them out. In 1819, they moved to Florissant, Missouri, nearer to St. Louis, where land had been purchased for them. Until their convent could be built, the sisters lived in a few primitive log cabins near the river. The convent was ready for their occupancy in 1820 and a nearby church the next year.

During her first ten years in the United States, Mother Duchesne and her sisters experienced all the hardships of frontier life except the threat of massacre by the Indians. They had to put up with primitive lodging in cramped quarters, shortages of food and drinking water, both the heat and cold of Missouri weather, and occasional forest fires. But they persevered and received their first American candidates for the community.

As other nuns arrived from France to complement the Americans, Mother Duchesne decided to expand their operations. In 1821 she sent two nuns to Opelousa, Louisiana, about 150 miles north of New Orleans, to establish the Grand Coteau convent, and she followed the next year.

That second journey on the Mississippi River turned out to be a nightmare. It took her from July 20 to August 29 to reach Grand Coteau and eighty days to return. On the trip back, yellow fever broke out on the riverboat on which she was traveling and it went ashore at Natchez. With the yellow fever scare, though, the citizens of Natchez wouldn't allow the passengers in the town and they had to get out on the opposite bank of the river. Mother Duchesne had been caring for the ill and she herself contracted a high fever. A Mrs. Davis received her hospitably but the only bed she could find was one in which a woman had just died of the fever.

Once she recovered enough to continue, she boarded another riverboat, but this one ran aground on a sandbank at New Madrid in southeastern Missouri and was stuck there for five days until the water rose enough to free the boat.

More convents were founded at St. Michael on the Mississippi River in 1825, in St. Louis in 1827, in St. Charles also in 1827, and at La Fourche, Louisiana in 1828. However, the one at La Fourche was closed four years later. With the convent in St. Louis, the sisters established an academy or boarding school for girls, an orphanage, and a day school. The boarders at Florissant were transferred to St. Louis and Mother Duchesne, who had been at Florissant for eight years, also moved to St. Louis. She was the superior there for the next seven years.

In 1829-1830, Mother Duchesne made a third trip on the Mississippi River to confer with the heads of the convents in Louisiana. This trip went smoother than the previous two. However, when she was returning after visiting Grand Coteau, St. Michael and La Fourche, she got only as far as the mouth of the Ohio River. She traveled the rest of the way back to St. Louis by oxcart.

At the time of her visitation to the convents in Louisiana, twelve years after she and the other four sisters came from France, the Society had six convents along the Mississippi River with 64 nuns. Fourteen of them had come from France and fifty were Americans. The sisters were teaching more than 350 children.

Mother Duchesne, however, was not satisfied. She still dreamed of working as an active missionary among the Indians rather than as the superior of the Sacred Heart nuns. She began to ask Mother Barat to relieve her of her duties but Mother Barat insisted that there was no one to take her place. Finally, in 1834,

Mother Barat appointed Mother Eugenie Aude as assistant mother general for America for the Society of the Sacred Heart, relieving Mother Duchesne of the leadership. Mother Duchesne was transferred back to Florissant where she served as superior of the novitiate convent for five years.

In 1839, at age seventy and in failing health, she returned to the convent in St. Louis. Her health improved, though, about the time that Father Pierre Jean De Smet, a missionary among the Indians of the northwestern United States, asked the sisters to set up a school for the Potawatomi Indians at Sugar Creek, in present-day Kansas. This was the fulfillment of the dream that Philippine had had since she was a little girl and she asked to be included. Her request was granted.

So on June 29, 1841, two months before her 72nd birthday, Mother Duchesne, three other Sacred Heart nuns, and three priests left St. Louis for Sugar Creek. They went by boat to Westport Landing, modern Kansas City, and then made a four-day journey by wagon. At the settlement, about 700 Indians assembled to welcome the sisters. One of the Indians vacated his house so the sisters could live there while their primitive home was being built.

The Potawatomi Indians had come from northern Indiana in 1835 when the U.S. government moved them from the eastern states to territory west of the Mississippi River. About half of the Indians were already Catholics and those who weren't were gradually converting to Catholicism.

While the sisters' convent was being constructed, Mother Duchesne was advised to spend most of her time in the church, which had been completed the previous year. Unable any more to do heavy work, and not understanding the Indians' language, she felt that she could at least pray for the success of the other sisters' work. She practically lived in the church and came to be known among the Indians as *Quah-kah-ka-num-ad*, Woman-who-prays-always. Indian children would sneak up behind her as she knelt and sprinkle bits of paper on her habit. When they came back hours later, they found them undisturbed.

In 1842, Mother Elizabeth Galitzin, official visitor of the American convents of the Society, arrived at Sugar Creek Mission. Recognizing how sick and feeble Mother Duchesne had become, she decided that it was time for her to retire to the convent in St. Charles. Disappointed, but resigned to God's will, Mother Duchesne returned to Missouri, arriving back in St. Louis exactly one year after she had left.

The remaining ten years of Mother Duchesne's life were, unfortunately, marred by controversy. When the sisters decided that they should close the convent at St. Charles, she campaigned against the decision and won; the convent was kept open. However, she was less successful in trying to keep the convent at Florissant open. It was closed so the sisters could concentrate their resources in nearby St. Louis.

Mother Duchesne tried to keep up a correspondence with Mother Barat in France, as she had always done, but for two years after she returned to St. Charles her letters went unanswered. One of the other sisters was confiscating the letters and they never reached Mother Barat. Nor did Mother Barat's letters reach Mother Duchesne. Mother Barat was puzzled that Mother Duchesne had stopped writing to her and she sent her niece to the United States to find out why. Communication was quickly restored between the two saintly friends.

During the last years of her life, Mother Duchesne edified all who knew her by her holy and prayerful life. After working for 34 years in the United States, she died peacefully at noon on November 18, 1852. She was 83.

Pope Pius XII beatified Rose Philippine Duchesne on May 12, 1940. Pope John Paul II canonized her on July 3, 1988. Her feast is celebrated on November 18.

CHAPTER 12

Blessed Theodore Guèrin

(1798-1856)

 While Rose Philippine Duchesne was facing the hardships of life in Missouri, another heroic and saintly nun was establishing a religious order in Indiana. Mother Theodore Guèrin, the foundress of the Sisters of Providence of Saint Mary-of-the-Woods, was a contemporary of Mother Duchesne, although younger. Mother Theodore died four years after Mother Duchesne did.

Both women grew up in France and both were nuns there before they came to America. Mother Theodore, though, came to the United States the same year that Mother Duchesne, at age 72, was finally realizing her dream of being a missionary among the Indians at Sugar Creek, Kansas.

Mother Theodore was born Anne-Thérèse Guèrin in the village of Etables in Brittany, France, on October 2, 1798 as the French Revolution was drawing to a close. She was the second child and first daughter of Laurent and Isabelle Lefevre Guèrin. Two more children would be born to the family, but two of the children—the firstborn son and the fourth child, also a son—died as children. Anne-Thérèse and her younger sister, Marie-Jeanne, survived.

Laurent was an officer in the French Navy and was away from home most of the time, leaving Isabelle to care for the children. Since it was dangerous in those days to practice their religion openly, Isabelle taught her daughters reading and catechism at home. However, Anne-Thérèse attended a small school in Etables for a short time and was taught by a former seminarian who lived with the Guèrin family for several months. She became a devout young girl and her spiritual development was sufficient enough that she was permitted to receive her First Communion when she was ten, two years earlier than normal in those days.

When Anne-Thérèse was fifteen, bandits murdered her father. This was more than Isabelle could take. She had already lost two sons, and now her husband. The intensity of her grief incapacitated her so much that Anne-Thérèse had to assume the responsibility of caring for her and Marie-Jeanne. When Marie-Jeanne became old enough to help care for their mother, Anne-Thérèse worked as a seamstress to support the family.

When she was twenty, Anne-Thérèse asked her mother for permission to join a religious order. Isabelle absolutely refused. She could not lose her daughter, too! It was another five years before Isabelle recovered from her grief enough to give Anne-Thérèse permission to follow her vocation.

She chose the Sisters of Providence, a new order in France founded by Father Jacques-François Dujarie. The French Revolution was now over, but few priests remained in France and the people were suffering from the effects of the revolution. His religious order would be devoted to teaching and working among the poor.

Anne-Thérèse entered the novitiate at Ruille on August 18, 1823, professed her first vows on September 8, 1825, and her perpetual vows on September 5, 1831. Anne-Thérèse chose Sister St. Theodore as her name in religion.

In 1825, while Anne-Thérèse was still a novice, Mother Mary Lecor, the order's superior, sent her to teach at Preuilly-sur-Claise. While she was there, she contracted a serious illness, probably

smallpox. In curing the sickness, the doctors damaged her diges-
tive system to such an extent that she could thereafter eat only a
simple, bland diet.

After she professed first vows, Sister St. Theodore was named
superior of the sisters' establishment in the parish of Saint Aubin
in a rough section of the town of Rennes. She was there for eight
years during which she honed her skills at teaching young girls,
skills that she was to remember all her life and that she would teach
to other sisters.

In 1834, Sister St. Theodore was transferred to Soulaines in
the Diocese of Angers, where she was superior of the sisters there.

In 1838, Father Celestine de la Hailandière arrived in Rennes
in search of a congregation of women willing to establish a mission in Indiana. Father de la Hailandière was a native of Rennes
who had been persuaded by Bishop Simon Gabriel Bruté, the
Bishop of Vincennes, Indiana, to become his vicar general in 1835.
The Diocese of Vincennes included the state of Indiana and the
eastern part of Illinois, 330 miles long and just as wide, with a population of about 600,000, of whom about 50,000 were Catholics.
When Bishop Bruté was looking for priests in 1835, there was only
one other priest, Father Simon Petit Lalumière, in the diocese.
Twenty priests responded to Bishop Bruté's request in 1835 for
more priests, including Father de la Hailandière, and in 1838 he
returned to France in search of sisters.

Bishop Bruté died on June 26, 1839 and Father de la Hailandière succeeded him. He was consecrated Bishop of Vincennes in
Paris on August 18 of that year.

When Bishop de la Hailandière spoke with the Sisters of
Providence about the need for sisters in the United States, Mother
Mary agreed to ask for volunteers to go to Indiana. Sister St.
Theodore did not volunteer. Unlike Rose Philippine Duchesne,
who had always dreamed of being a missionary, Sister St. Theodore
had no such dream. She feared that her fragile health might hinder
the mission and didn't feel capable of leading it. Encouraged,
though, by Mother Mary and the bishops of Rennes and Le Mans,

and after long hours of prayer and reflection, she agreed to go. She had, after all, taken a vow of obedience and the rule of the congregation stated that "sisters will be disposed to go to whatsoever part of the world obedience calls them."

Sister St. Theodore and five other sisters left Ruille on July 12, 1840 for what proved to be a hazardous journey to the wilderness of Indiana. The journey took more than three months. Their ship was almost destroyed several times by a hurricane and other severe storms and Sister St. Theodore's diary described the feeling of "passing the night in the bottom of a vessel, hearing continually the dreadful creaking which makes one fear that it will split open." After another storm, she wrote, "Nothing was heard on board but screams and lamentations."

Finally reaching New York on September 4, she wrote, "We threw ourselves on our knees with hearts full of gratitude." But their problems weren't over yet. The sisters had expected a representative of Bishop de la Hailandière to meet the ship, but he was not there. None of the sisters could speak English and they had no idea how to get to Indiana. A doctor who boarded the ship with customs officials took pity on them and said that he would contact the bishop of New York about their plight.

The next day a priest took them to Brooklyn where they stayed with a woman accustomed to caring for missionaries when they first arrived in the United States. A man who spoke French then accompanied them to Philadelphia, where they stayed with the Sisters of Charity. There they met a French priest who was himself going to Vincennes, and they were welcome to accompany him.

They traveled by train, stagecoach, and steamboat, and finally reached Madison, Indiana. There they met Bishop de la Hailandière, who told them that they were to be settled near Terre Haute. Another steamboat took them to Evansville, Indiana, and then a stagecoach to Vincennes. From there a Father Buteux, assigned as chaplain for the sisters, accompanied them through roadless forests and across the Wabash River to Terre Haute and then on to

Saint Mary-of-the-Woods. At one point on the journey, their stage-coach overturned in a mud hole.

On October 22, 1840, as Sister St. Theodore was to record later, "We continued to advance into the thick woods until suddenly Father Buteux stopped the carriage and said, 'Come down, Sisters, we have arrived.' What was our astonishment to find ourselves still in the midst of the forest, no village, not even a house in sight."

They were led down into a ravine from which they could see a frame house and some sheds on the other side. This was to be their home, deep in the woods. Sister St. Theodore could only wonder how it would ever be possible to establish a novitiate and a school in this remote forest.

There were four postulants waiting for the sisters, so the community now consisted of ten women. On the instructions of Bishop de la Hailandière, the sisters began calling Sister St. Theodore "Mother Theodore," the title she would keep the rest of her life. The sisters began studying English and Mother Theodore instructed the postulants in the way of religious life.

On Christmas night of 1840, Mother Theodore became critically ill, suffering from fever, severe headaches, and periods of unconsciousness. The illness continued for almost two months and she continued to have poor health the rest of her life.

After she recovered to some extent, Mother Theodore began to plan her academy for girls. By the end of July 1841 ten young women were studying at Saint Mary-of-the-Woods. The following March the sisters opened a school in Jasper, Indiana and in October 1842 two sisters were sent to St. Francisville, Illinois.

During the years that followed, the sisters had numerous trials, of all kinds. They suffered from hunger, sometimes going without food for days. They experienced the heat, humidity and mosquitoes of Indiana summers, and the cold and heavy snow of the winters. They planted crops and raised hogs and other animals on their farm, and were beginning to have a bit more to eat, when a fire destroyed their barn and harvest. The sisters were also short of money and Bishop de la Hailandière refused to support them. He suggested that Mother Theodore go back to France to raise money for the community.

In 1843, she did return to France and was gone for eleven months. She was successful in raising money, and also in clarifying the relationship between the sisters in the United States and those in France. Mother Theodore's return trip to Indiana was nearly as difficult as her first journey there. Her ship again experienced bad weather and she was ill when she reached New Orleans. Her health continued to be very frail.

Mother Theodore's greatest problem from 1843 to 1847, though, concerned her relationship with Bishop de la Hailandière. Even before she left for France it was clear that the bishop believed that he possessed total control over the Sisters of Providence, despite what the community's rule said. Mother Theodore often had to oppose his decisions as they affected her community, always doing so as respectfully as possible.

While she was in France, Bishop de la Hailandière took over the community. He admitted novices to vows, closed the school at St. Francisville, received three nuns from another community, opened a new establishment, and called for the election of a new superior—all without input from the sisters and contrary to the community's rule. He hoped that the sisters would elect a different superior, but they reelected Mother Theodore.

After her return, her meetings with Bishop de la Hailandière grew more and more contentious, often lasting for hours. Sometimes the bishop berated her for her leadership of the community and other times he insisted that he did not want to be involved in the affairs of the community. The diocese still owned the property at Saint Mary-of-the-Woods and at times the bishop would promise to give it to the sisters and other times would refuse to do so. He insisted on an "Act of Reparation" from the sisters because he believed that they had spoken out against him to his superiors.

The matter reached its climax in 1847 when Bishop de la Hailandière declared that Mother Theodore was no longer the superior. Furthermore, he told her, she was no longer a Sister of Providence. He released her from her vows and demanded that she leave his diocese.

It was precisely at this point that the Vatican appointed a new bishop for the Diocese of Vincennes. Mother Theodore wasn't the only one who was having difficulties with Bishop de la Hailandière. So were many of the diocesan priests. Amid the turmoil in the diocese, Bishop de la Hailandière submitted his resignation to the Vatican.

The Vatican accepted his resignation on July 16, 1847 and appointed John Stephen Bazin the Bishop of Vincennes. Bishop de la Hailandière returned to France, where he lived another 35 years before his death in 1882. Bishop Bazin was consecrated bishop of the diocese on October 24 and one of his first acts was to deliver a valid deed to the property at Saint Mary-of-the-Woods to Mother Theodore.

Bishop Bazin was able to restore peace and harmony to the Diocese of Vincennes. However, he died only six months after his consecration. Seven months later, Jacques M. Maurice Landes d'Aussac de Saint-Palais was named Bishop of Vincennes and he, too, supported the sisters without interfering in their work. After discovering the pitiful condition of the building used as the sisters' motherhouse, he promised financial assistance so the sisters could erect a new building. A three-story brick structure with basement was built, and the sisters occupied it in 1853.

Mother Theodore was finally able to devote all her energies to building and nurturing her congregation, and establishing schools. She made annual visits by steamship and stagecoach over very bad roads to all the establishments, which included parish schools in ten cities in Indiana and one in Illinois. In 1855, the community that began with six sisters fifteen years before had increased to sixty. The sisters were teaching 1,200 children, and also operated two orphanages. Between visits to the establishments, she kept up a large correspondence with the sisters there.

But her health continued to get worse. She died during the early morning hours of May 14, 1856 at the age of 57. Pope John Paul II beatified her on October 25, 1998, 200 years and 23 days after her birth.

Today about 650 Sisters of Providence of Saint Mary-of-the-Woods operate Saint Mary-of-the-Woods College, where the motherhouse is located. They have touched tens of thousands of lives through their various ministries in the United States as well as in Taiwan, China, South America, and the West Indies.

CHAPTER 13

Saint John Neumann

(1811-1860)

John Neumann beat Mother Theodore Guèrin to the United States by four years. He, however, was only 25 when he arrived. She was 42. She came from France, he from Bohemia. Both were to accomplish great things in their adopted country.

John was born on March 28, 1811 in the town of Prachatitz, Bohemia, which is now part of the Czech Republic but then was part of Austria. When he was baptized the day he was born, he was given the same name as the patron saint of the Czechs and Slovaks, John Nepomucene, or "of Nepomuk." He was the third of six children of Philip and Agnes Lebis Neumann. His father was a Bavarian who moved to Prachatitz in 1802 when Napoleon Bonaparte's army overran Europe. Agnes was Philip's second wife, his first wife having died in childbirth along with her child.

John was always small, as a child and as an adult, when he was only five feet two inches tall. He took after his father in his love of reading, and was a good student. He enrolled in the gymnasium—a high school and college—when he was twelve and graduated when he was twenty. Then, attracted to the priesthood, he entered the diocesan seminary at nearby Budweis. He studied there and at the archdiocesan seminary in Prague, distinguishing himself as a serious student. He mastered theology and also became fluent in Latin, Greek, Hebrew and eight modern languages, including various Slavic dialects.

In 1835 he was ready to be ordained to the priesthood, having received minor orders. Major orders, however, were put off, first because of the illness of the Bishop of Budweis and then indefinitely because (a reason we find difficult to believe today) the diocese thought it had a sufficient number of priests.

Since John was not needed as a priest in Bohemia, be looked elsewhere. He learned about the work of missionaries in the United States and became enthused about going there. He left Prachatitz on February 8, 1836, without saying good-bye to his parents. He thought that it would be easier for all if he would write a farewell letter to them after he left, which he did from Budweis.

As was usually the case for those who went to America from Europe, his passage was difficult. First he made his way across Europe on foot, by stagecoach and boat, arriving at Le Havre, France on April 7. He booked passage on the *Europa*, a large three-mast ship, at the cheapest rate possible, which meant that he was allowed to place a thin straw mattress and pillow wherever he could find a vacant spot on the crowded deck. The ship left Le Havre on April 20, 1836 and arrived in New York's harbor six weeks later, on June 2. On the way it sailed through four days of raging storms, had to wait out a calm, and evaded dangerous icebergs. After it arrived in New York's harbor, it had to stay there for another week in quarantine before passengers were allowed to disembark on Staten Island and go through customs.

It was pouring down rain when John reached Manhattan, shabbily dressed and with only a few francs in his pocket. He slept in a small inn that night. The next day he learned where the bishop's residence was, and he went there. Those at the residence were a bit dubious when John introduced himself, especially because of his shabby appearance, but he was finally admitted. Bishop John Dubois, the third bishop of New York, was pleased to see a man who aspired to become a priest in his diocese because he had only 36 priests to care for the 200,000 Catholics who were then living in his diocese which comprised all of New York State and half of New Jersey. It was far different from the situation in Bohemia.

Since John had papers that showed that he had already received minor orders and was ready for major orders, Bishop Dubois ordained him a sub-deacon on June 19, a deacon on June 24, and a priest on June 25. A few days later, wearing a new suit given to him by another priest, Father Neumann was on his way to his first assignment, in Buffalo. He was to be assistant there to Father Pax, the pastor.

The parish consisted of 900 square miles in western New York and Father Pax had been the only priest, so he was happy indeed to welcome the new priest. He suggested that they divide the work by having one priest stay in Buffalo and the other care for the outlying areas, and he offered Father Neumann his choice. John chose the country districts and made his headquarters at Williamsville, eight miles northeast of Buffalo, where there was an unfinished stone church.

He had about 400 parishioners, 300 of them of German ancestry and the rest Irish, French and Scottish. Father Neumann already spoke German, of course, and he soon learned to speak English and even Gaelic. He and his parishioners finished constructing the church.

He remained there only a year, though, before moving to another town that had a log-cabin church. He built a two-room log cabin for himself and lived in it very austerely, seldom building a fire even in the cold winters of upstate New York. He ate a meager diet, sometimes only bread and water. He walked to other towns in the parish, sometimes thirty or forty miles away, in all kinds of weather, saying Mass for parishioners in other log chapels.

This was still Indian country and once, when Father Neumann lay down under a tree for a rest, he awoke to find himself surrounded by menacing Indians. He immediately got on his knees and started to pray. The Indians then realized he was a priest and became friendly, putting him on a buffalo skin and carrying him to his destination.

A parishioner gave him a horse that he used on longer journeys. However, it was a spirited horse and Father Neumann had trouble controlling it, so he preferred to walk.

When Bishop Dubois visited during the summer of 1837 to administer the sacrament of Confirmation, he was surprised to see how much the little priest had accomplished in such a short time.

Father Neumann couldn't keep up his pace for long, though. He began to suffer from fevers and then, at Easter time in 1840, he had a complete breakdown. When he recovered, he decided to become a Redemptorist priest. The Congregation of the Most Holy Redeemer (Redemptorists) was founded by Alphonsus Liguori, who had just been canonized in 1839. Father Neumann had visited their house in Rochester three times and was favorably impressed with what he saw. He formally applied for admission to the congregation and was accepted.

On instructions from the Redemptorists' superior, Father Neumann crossed Lake Erie and went to Pittsburgh. There he was invested with the religious habit on November 29, 1840, becoming the first novice of the Redemptorists in the United States. He spent his novitiate year preaching missions in cities in a wide area of the eastern United States: Baltimore, New York, Rochester, Buffalo, Norwalk, and three places in Ohio—Canton, Randolph and Steubenville. At Steubenville, his illness recurred.

He returned to Baltimore in December and made his religious profession on January 16, 1842. Then, as a professed Redemptorist, he continued his missionary work despite the fact that he suffered constantly from poor health. He worked principally among the Germans and became popular among them.

He was also appointed to important positions within the Redemptorists, first as one of two consultors to the American superior, then superior in Pittsburgh from 1843 to 1846. While in Pittsburgh, he wrote both a small and a large German catechism and a German Bible history, both of which were published. He also began work on a comprehensive work on theology, but he never completed it.

While he was superior in Pittsburgh, one of his priests was Father Francis Xavier Seelos, who is profiled in the next chapter. Father Seelos' description of the relationship between the two priests, and the type of man Father Neumann was at the time, is included in that chapter.

In 1847 Father Neumann was appointed vice-regent of the American Redemptorists and, in 1848, vice-provincial and superior of the congregation in Baltimore. He was replaced as vice-provincial in 1849 but continued as superior in Baltimore. He was also rector of St. Alphonsus Church in Baltimore.

In 1851, the Vatican appointed Bishop Francis Patrick Kenrick, the bishop of Philadelphia, to the see of Baltimore. The new archbishop recommended Father Neumann as his successor in Philadelphia. Father Neumann tried to refuse the appointment and accepted it only because Pope Pius IX commanded him to do so. He was consecrated the fourth bishop of Philadelphia on March 28, 1852, when he was 41. For his motto he chose the words, "Passion of Christ, strengthen me."

Later in 1852, the U.S. bishops held the First Plenary Council of Baltimore and, of course, Bishop Neumann attended. He was asked to revise the catechism he wrote while he was in Pittsburgh. It appeared a year later as an approved textbook of 180 pages and it continued to be used widely throughout the United States for most of the rest of the nineteenth century.

Bishop Neumann then settled down to administer his vast diocese, the largest in the United States at the time. It included eastern Pennsylvania, western New Jersey, and all of Delaware. The bishop made it a point to visit the larger parishes in the diocese once a year, and the smaller ones every other year. He usually stayed in the parishes for several days saying Mass, preaching, confirming, hearing confessions, and visiting the sick.

He was the first to introduce the Forty Hours Devotion in

the United States, a devotion that was popular in most places until the Second Vatican Council. In 1853 he produced a Latin brochure that contained the prayers and rubrics for the devotion.

Above all, Bishop Neumann is known for his administrative abilities and for his leadership in organizing the parochial school system. When he arrived in Philadelphia in 1852 there were two Catholic schools. Eight years later there were nearly 100. To staff them, he attracted to the diocese a number of teaching orders of both men and women religious, including the Christian Brothers for boys and the Notre Dame Sisters of Munich and the Holy Cross Sisters of France for girls. He founded the Sisters of the Third Order of St. Francis, Philadelphia Foundation and was a patron of the Colored Oblate Sisters of Baltimore, saving that order from extinction.

In the course of only five years, Bishop Neumann saw fifty churches erected in the diocese. He began the building of the magnificent cathedral and saw its exterior completed. He raised the standards of studies at Saint Charles Borromeo Seminary in Ellicott, Maryland, and founded a diocesan preparatory seminary.

Despite the time it required to administer his diocese, Bishop Neumann also found time to write, including articles for the Philadelphia newspapers.

In 1854 Bishop Neumann went to Rome to be present when Pope Pius IX solemnly proclaimed the doctrine of the Immaculate Conception. While in Rome, he had a private audience with the pope during which he was able to report that, in less than three years, the number of children in the diocese's parochial schools had increased from 500 to 9,000. The pope is reported to have smiled and said, "Bishop Neumann of Philadelphia, is not obedience better than sacrifice?"

During the Eighth Provincial Council of Baltimore in 1855, the bishops discussed the possibility of dividing the Diocese of Philadelphia. Bishop Neumann was wholly in favor of this because of the tremendous work involved in administering such a large diocese, and favored the erection of a Diocese of Pottsville. He also offered to go there if the diocese were divided because he felt more comfortable working among the people in rural areas than in Philadelphia. Pottsville was never made a diocese, but in 1857 the Vatican appointed a coadjutor bishop for the Diocese of Philadelphia. He was Bishop James Frederick Wood, a native of Philadelphia.

During the Ninth Provincial Council of Baltimore in 1858, the bishops returned to the subject of dividing the diocese and, once again, Bishop Neumann volunteered to be transferred there, leaving Bishop Wood in charge of Philadelphia. During the discussion, some of the bishops misunderstood Bishop Neumann and thought that he wanted to resign from the episcopacy. Indeed, this was the common impression among the bishops because Bishop Neumann spoke so often of his ineptitude and unworthiness to be a bishop, undoubtedly his true feelings despite all that he had accomplished as a bishop. This word reached the Vatican and Bishop Neumann was asked to clarify the matter.

Realizing that there was a misunderstanding, Bishop Neumann explained the matter in a letter to Cardinal Barnabo at the Congregation for the Doctrine of the Faith. He wrote that he did not want to resign but if he had done something that displeased the pope, he would leave the episcopacy without any hesitation. He explained, "It seemed to me that my character was little suited for the very cultural world of Philadelphia. I am much more accustomed to the country, and will be able to care for the people and faithful living in the mountains, in the coal mines and on the farms" if he were transferred to Pottsville or Wilmington, North Carolina. He wrote that he was willing either to remain in Philadelphia or to resign from the episcopacy and ended his letter, "I desire nothing but to fulfill the wish of the Holy Father whatever it may be."

It's impossible to know whether he might have been transferred to a more rural diocese because Bishop Neumann died suddenly on January 8, 1860 when he was only 48 years old. He was taking care of some business matters when he suffered a stroke in front of a private residence. He was taken into the house, where he died.

Pope Paul VI beatified him on October 13, 1963 and canonized him on June 19, 1977, so far the only North American bishop to be canonized. His feast day is celebrated on January 5.

CHAPTER 14

Blessed Francis Xavier Seelos

(*1819-1867*)

In 1844, while Father John Neumann was superior of the Redemptorist Fathers in Pittsburgh, Pennsylvania, one of his priests was a 25-year-old man named Francis Xavier Seelos. Father Seelos was newly ordained and enthusiastic about his assignment to help with the spiritual care of some of the 45,000 Catholics in western Pennsylvania. Of course, neither Father Neumann nor Father Seelos knew that both of them would one day be recognized as American saints, Neumann canonized and Seelos beatified.

Like John Neumann, Francis Seelos was an immigrant to the United States. He was born in Fussen, Germany on January 11, 1819, the sixth of Mang and Frances Seelos' nine children. When Francis was born, Mang was in the cloth-weaving business, but the business failed and Mang supported his family on the wages paid to him as a church sacristan.

Mang and Frances were deeply religious and they tried to instill this quality in their children. Mass, prayers around the dinner table, and spiritual reading were part of the daily routine. The spiritual reading always included something on the life of the saint whose feast day was being celebrated, and it was thus that Francis learned about his patron saint, Francis Xavier. Even as a child, Francis spoke about becoming a missionary like the sixteenth-century Jesuit.

When he was old enough, Francis became an altar server in his parish church. The pastor, Father Francis Anton Heim, took an interest in him and arranged for him to attend high school in Augsburg and to receive his higher education at the University of Munich. He was a popular student at the university, joining a fraternity and taking fencing and dancing lessons. He also loved to sing but, according to his classmates, always at the top of his lungs. He apparently startled other worshipers at Mass by singing louder than anyone else did.

While at the University of Munich, Francis still planned to become a Jesuit, or perhaps a diocesan priest. But in 1842 the Redemptorist Fathers were appealing for missionaries to go to the United States. The Redemptorists had begun sending missionaries to the United States in 1833 and they explained to their listeners how badly priests were needed there. One day in 1842, Francis told his brother Adam, "Last night the Blessed Mother appeared to me. I have to become a missionary." He left the university and sent a letter of application to the superior of the Redemptorists in the United States.

When a reply to his application didn't come immediately, Francis entered the Augsburg diocesan seminary. The letter of acceptance arrived three weeks later.

Francis and three other Redemptorists arrived in New York on April 20, 1843. He was sent to the Redemptorist novitiate at Saint James Parish in Baltimore where he completed his novitiate and training. He was ordained to the priesthood on December 22, 1844. He remained in Baltimore for eight months assisting at Saint James Parish, and then was assigned to Saint Philomena's Church in Pittsburgh, where, as already noted, he came under the influence of Father John Neumann.

This influence was considerable. Here is what Father Seelos wrote about their relationship: "I was his subject but more like a son who needed help, for I had just left the novitiate and was inexperienced. In every respect he was a remarkable father to me. He introduced me to the practical life; he guided me as my spiritual leader and confessor. He cared for all my needs in body and soul; above all, the example of his virtues is vivid in my memory, his tender modesty, his great humility, and his insuperable patience.

"Our dwelling was so poor that one night we had to leave our room in a severe storm and seek protection elsewhere, because the water was pouring down on our beds. I say our room because we were in one and the same room, which was separated only by a curtain. For that reason I could hear him often saying his prayers during the night. He slept so little that I could not understand how he could keep his body and soul together. Because he generally got up before the regular rising time, he prepared the fire, often bringing up coal himself to have the room warm for me when I got up."

Father Seelos immediately began performing the duties of a priest—offering Mass, preaching, performing weddings and funerals, visiting the sick, and hearing confessions.

Soon he became known for his preaching, which he could do in three languages—German, French, and English, although the English was heavily accented. The content of his sermons was conventional enough, but his manner of delivering them was highly unconventional. He began to act out Scripture narratives with extended imaginary conversations with Jesus, his apostles, and other characters in the Scriptures. During the conversations, "Jesus" would turn to the congregation and make wry observations about the Gospel passage—sometimes quite humorous. Father Seelos spent hours preparing these sermons, writing them out and practicing their delivery.

Midway through the sermons, Father Seelos would stop for a suitable period of time to change the mood. Then he would continue in a more serious tone of voice and explain the points he had made during his play-acting. He would conclude with an exhortation to the people to come to him in confession, promising to receive them "with all mildness." It was highly effective and the lines outside his confessional would wind around the church and some-times out the door. During an era when priests were sometimes harsh with penitents, Father Seelos always received them with kindness.

During the years between 1854 and 1862, Father Seelos served two communities in Maryland. He was pastor and religious superior in Saint Alphonsus Parish in Baltimore from 1854 to 1857, and pastor, superior, prefect of students, and professor at Saints Peter and Paul Parish in Cumberland from 1857 to 1862. In one of his letters to his sister while he was pastor of Saint Alphonsus Church in Baltimore, he described his busy life: "I cannot thank God enough for my vocation, although from morning till night I am overwhelmed with cares and worries.... White and black, Ger-man and English, confreres and externs, clerical and lay people, aristocratic women and unworldly nuns, the poor, the sick, ask for my assistance. One wants this, the other than. There is no rest. It takes a real effort to snatch a little time for spiritual reading or a visit to the Blessed Sacrament. Could I write you an account of the experiences of even one day, you would be astonished."

Soon stories about his dedication began to spread. His confreres reported that he routinely went to bed at night fully clothed, except for his shoes, and that he slept on a bench near the front door so that he could respond quickly if someone arrived who needed the services of a priest.

He made the anti-Catholic newspapers in Baltimore after he responded to a late-night appeal from prostitutes to minister to a young woman who was dying. He stayed with the prostitute until she died. When the newspapers insinuated that he remained in the house for other purposes, Father Seelos said simply, "Let the fel-lows talk on. I saved a soul."

On a cold winter day, Father Seelos passed a destitute man on the street. Seeing the rags tied around his feet, Father Seelos sat on the curb, took off the boots he was wearing, gave them to the man, wished him well, and walked on in his stockings.

Father Seelos considered visiting the sick a particularly important part of his work. During those visits, he said the usual prayers for the sick. Then he would pull up a chair, visit with the sick person for a while, and read passages of a book. Once when he was visiting a sick woman, he gathered up the family's dirty laundry and took it back to his rectory where he washed and mended it.

He always found time to visit lonely people despite their circumstances. At times, though, his confreres considered him to be "scandalously wasting time" and criticized him for it. He replied, "I do nothing wrong in receiving all kindly, without distinction. It would be wrong to receive some affably and some rudely."

The middle 1800's was a time of rampant anti-Catholicism in the United States and priests literally took their lives in their hands when they traveled alone. Nevertheless, Father Seelos sometimes traveled up to 100 miles to visit Catholic families. During his trips, at one time or another, he was pelted with rocks, beaten, threatened at gunpoint, and nearly thrown overboard while on a ferry.

In 1857 the pace of Father Seelos' life began to take its toll on his health. One day blood spurted from his mouth. The doctor who examined him found that he had broken a blood vessel in his throat and ordered him to bed. After his throat healed, the provincial reassigned him to the smaller church in Cumberland. Here he was happy to serve as a father figure and mentor in his role as prefect of students and professor.

Father Seelos was in Cumberland when the Civil War began. There were two incidents involving the Redemptorist seminary. First there was a false rumor that guns and ammunition were being hidden there, prompting a forced search. Then, in August of 1861, when seminarians were playing a game near the Virginia border, they were mistaken for an attacking army.

In 1862, with war seeming to get closer and closer, Father Seelos and the students moved to Annapolis, Maryland. He was appointed pastor of Saint Mary's Parish, religious superior and prefect of students at the adjoining seminary. The Redemptorist seminary was on property that was formerly the estate of Charles Carroll of Carrollton, the only Catholic signer of the Declaration of Independence.

In 1863, President Abraham Lincoln signed the Conscription Act that stipulated that all men twenty to 45 years of age could be drafted. Father Seelos was afraid that his seminarians might be drafted, and he himself was 44, so he went to Washington to talk with the president about the draft. Lincoln received him kindly but did not assure him that the students would be exempt from the draft. It turned out, though, that none of them were drafted.

Unfortunately, some of his fellow Redemptorist priests did not always appreciate Father Seelos. Some of them, in fact, spent an inordinate amount of time and effort sending official complaints to his superiors about what they considered his defects. Among the complaints were that he was "wretchedly weak," "an old mother," "a blockhead," and "wanting in wisdom and foresight." While he was prefect of Redemptorist students, official complaints were filed that he lacked experience, insight, and firmness, and that he could not speak Latin well. It didn't go over well with some of the other priests when Father Seelos permitted the students to play music after night prayers, swim at a beach, and put on school plays.

The complainants were successful. His superiors declared Father Seelos unfit to direct the sixty students then in religious formation and they took his position as prefect of students away from him. He was appointed superior of the Redemptorist mission band and for the next three years he traveled from parish to parish giving missions—a carefully prepared program of sermons and spiritual exercises. He preached missions in Missouri, Illinois, Wisconsin, Michigan, Ohio, Pennsylvania, New York, New Jersey, Connecticut, and Rhode Island. In a letter to his sister, he wrote, "I love the work of the missions more than anything else. It is properly *the* work in the vineyard of the Lord; it is entirely apostolic work."

His superiors then transferred him to Saint Mary's Parish in Detroit, where he assisted in parish ministry for ten months. Then, on September 27, 1866, he was transferred to Saint Mary's Assumption Parish in New Orleans. On the train going to New Orleans, a nun asked him how long he was going to be in New Orleans, and Father Seelos answered calmly, "For one year and then I'll die of yellow fever."

The other Redemptorist priests in New Orleans, most of whom had been Father Seelos' students in formation, welcomed him heartily, and he was happy to be there. By this time, Father Seelos had a wide reputation as a holy man. He continued to minister to all who wanted him and there were reports of remarkable conversions and cures following his visits.

In 1867, a severe outbreak of yellow fever seized New Orleans. A full one-third of the city's population of 150,000 contracted the disease, and 5,000 died. Father Seelos walked a considerable distance one day to visit a man with the disease, and he ministered to him until he died. By the time he got back to the rectory, he was so weak that he tumbled into bed. At first it was thought that he had only a mild form of yellow fever, but then one of his lungs collapsed, he lost his appetite, and became delirious.

His illness lasted for three weeks, with the New Orleans newspapers publishing regular updates on his condition. When he died on October 4, 1867, at age 48, his death made front-page news. He was buried in the crypt of Saint Mary's Assumption Church.

Pope John Paul II beatified him on April 9, 2000.

CHAPTER 15

Blessed Damien de Veuster

(1840-1889)

The reader may decide whether Damien de Veuster, the "leper priest," should be included among the saints and the blesseds of America. He was a Belgian who never set foot on the American continents. He performed the work for which he became famous, and for which he was beatified, in Hawaii during the nineteenth century, well before the Hawaiian Islands became part of the United States. He is included in this book because he is a Hawaiian hero and Hawaii is now an American state.

Like Junípero Serra, a large statue of Damien de Veuster is in Statuary Hall in the U.S. Capitol in Washington, D.C. It is one of the two statues for the state of Hawaii.

Damien de Veuster was born on January 3, 1840 in Tremelo, near Leuven, the Dutch-speaking part of Belgium. He was the seventh of eight children of Franciscus (or Frans) and Anne-Catherine (or Cato) Wouters de Veuster. When he was baptized on the day of his birth, he was given the name Joseph but was always familiarly known as Jef.

Jef's mother was apparently something of a shrew, hot-tempered and occasionally violent with her children. The neighbors whispered that she was a witch. She nevertheless made sure the children learned, and practiced, their religion. She read to them about the lives of saints. Saints that Jef particularly admired were the twins Cosmas and Damien, doctors who did many good deeds before dying as martyrs early in the fourth century. Five of the de Veuster children followed religious vocations.

Jef was a stubborn and mischievous child. In school he often had to sit in the front of the class wearing a dunce cap. He was sent to the École Commerciale (business school) where other students teased him because he couldn't speak French. He lashed back at them and gained a reputation as a bully. He also learned to speak French.

One day when Jef heard a Redemptorist priest preach a sermon, he got the message that he would burn in hell if he didn't follow his calling. At the time, the cult of the Sacred Hearts of Jesus and Mary was popular and Jef thought that his calling was to join the Order of the Sacred Hearts. He entered the order on his nineteenth birthday and made his provisional vows on February 2, 1859. At that time he took the name Damien after the saint he learned about as a child. He began studies for the priesthood in Paris and made final vows in the order on October 7, 1861.

While he was studying for the priesthood, Bishop Etienne Jaussen of Tahiti preached to the seminarians about missionary work in Tahiti. Damien's brother Auguste, already ordained a priest and known as Father Pamphile, signed up to go to Hawaii but became ill and the doctor declared him unfit to travel. Damien asked to take his place, pointing out that the order had already paid a thousand French francs for Pamphile's passage. Permission was granted and Damien, along with two French brothers, left Paris on October 28, 1863. Damien wrote a farewell letter to his parents asking them to pray that he would have the courage to carry out God's will.

The voyage to Hawaii took 4½ months. Damien stepped ashore in Honolulu on March 19, 1863. He was 23 years old and he would never leave Hawaii again.

Captain Cook had discovered Hawaii for Europeans in 1778. He was murdered there in 1779. Shortly after that, the Hawaiian Kamehameha, with the help of British sailors who had married Hawaiian women, started an uprising and from 1810 ruled the entire archipelago. Poor white settlers established a trade for ships. They also taught the Hawaiians to drink and smoke and introduced prostitution into the relaxed sexual world of the Polynesians. Venereal diseases soon followed, and so did leprosy, which most doctors at the time thought was the fourth stage of syphilis. The Polynesian people were dying out. There were about 300,000 Polynesians on the island when Captain Cook arrived and it had fallen to 70,000 in 1853, the rest having been wiped out by various diseases brought by the Europeans.

Missionaries began going to the Hawaiian Islands in 1820. They brought Christian values with them and taught the children of the Hawaiian chiefs. At the time Damien arrived in 1864, there were eighteen priests on the islands, many becoming elderly. About a third of the population was Catholic.

Damien was ordained a priest on May 21, 1864 in Honolulu's cathedral and was sent to the Big Island, Hawaii, near the active volcano there. The 350 Catholics in the area had not had a priest for years and Damien's first job was to build a church. It was the first of several churches he was to build with his own hands. He impressed the Hawaiians with his hardiness and willingness to share their way of life. He was constantly in the saddle, visiting the various communities.

On January 3, 1865 an event occurred that was to change Damien's life. The Hawaiian parliament passed an Act for the Combating of Leprosy. The disease was rampant on the islands and the new law required the Board of Health to establish an isolation area for lepers to which those with advanced cases of the disease were to be exiled. The Board of Health bought a piece of land on a peninsula on the northern coast of Molokai Island for that purpose. A wall of rock 600 meters high divided the leper colony from the rest of the island. The Pacific Ocean was on the remaining three sides. The place was isolated. On January 6, 1866, the first twelve people were exiled there.

However, all this did not immediately affect Father Damien, who was busy on the Big Island of Hawaii. He was there on April 2, 1868 when the nearby Kilauea volcano erupted, when a tidal wave reduced houses and his church to rubble, and when hurricanes caused much damage. Damien wrote that he found his life as a missionary difficult for these reasons and because of "the daily contact with a sinful world."

In 1873, ten years after he arrived in Hawaii, Damien went to Maui for a church consecration. Bishop Louis Maigret was present and, at one point, he asked Father Aubert Bouillon to report on the situation at the leper colony on Molokai. In doing so, Father Bouillon stressed the need for a priest there because the lepers were dying without spiritual support. When Bishop Maigret asked for volunteers, Damien and three others raised their hands. Bishop Maigret suggested that each of the four spend three months at a time with the exiles, and he chose Damien to go first. He arrived at the leper settlement on May 9, 1873.

At first the lepers in the settlement nauseated Damien. The hospital was new and clean but there was the constant stench of rotting flesh and diarrhea. The people coughed constantly, cleared their throats and spat on the ground. At Communion time during Mass, he felt repugnance at putting hosts on the infected tongues and he had to turn away to keep from getting sick. Damien, though, felt no desire to leave. He had found his life's work among these pitiful people. He wrote to his provincial, "I wish to sacrifice myself for the poor lepers. The harvest here seems ripe."

When Damien arrived, there were about 500 patients and 200 healthy people in the settlement, including 210 Catholics and twenty candidates for baptism. He soon realized that by following the policy he was instructed to follow, of no physical contact with the lepers, he was not winning their confidence. What good was it, he asked his superiors, to spend his life in the leper colony if he couldn't win the hearts of the lepers? He began to live freely among the people, truly sharing their way of life. He began his sermons with, "We lepers," although he was not—yet—afflicted with the disease.

Damien did not leave Molokai after three months. He remained for almost sixteen years, completely dedicated to his lepers. He not only cared for their spiritual needs but also did everything he could to improve their lives physically. It was in that regard that he frequently had disagreements with his superiors, both Bishop Hermann Kockemann (who succeeded Bishop Maigret) and the provincial of his Order, Father Leonor Fouesnel. Damien campaigned for more doctors and nurses, and for more priests. He was especially concerned that he often had to go for many months without being able to go to confession because other priests visited the peninsula infrequently.

Priests were occasionally sent to Molokai, including some who had contracted leprosy. Invariably, there would soon be disagreements that resulted in the priests being reassigned to other places. Damien was not an easy man to live with.

Damien got along better with Hawaiian royalty. Queen Liliuokalani was always an important source of support and King Kalakaua visited the settlement in 1874. Damien told the king that the exiles needed clothing and food supplies, and he explained the emotional problems they had with confinement. Damien also asked for the power to solemnize marriages so that the exiles could lead as normal a life as possible, a power he had not had before. The king gave orders for the priest to be granted these powers. This became a source of controversy because some of the lepers who married had been previously married to healthy partners who did not follow them to Molokai.

Through the years Damien made progress in the settlement. Meanwhile, he kept up a correspondence with his brother Pamphile, explaining what he was doing in Molokai. Pamphile took it upon himself to publish some of the letters in Belgium and soon Father Damien became famous. The publication of a long scientific article by American doctor George Woods, who had visited the settlement and seen Damien's work, made Damien internationally famous in medical circles in 1876. All this publicity, though, antagonized Damien's superiors who felt that Damien was not accomplishing everything single-handed, as he was being given credit for doing.

In 1881, Queen Liliuokalani honored Damien by making him a Knight Commander of the Royal Order of Kalakaua in recognition of his work. This served only to increase the jealousy felt by Damien's superiors.

In 1884, Charles Stoddard, a professor of English at the University of Notre Dame, visited Molokai. He went away greatly impressed with Damien and wrote a best-selling book about him. The book was translated into many languages. The magazine *Ave Maria*, published at Notre Dame, also spread Father Damien's fame—to the chagrin of his religious superiors, as did Robert Louis Stevenson who immortalized one of Father Damien's most vicious critics, Dr. Charles McEwen Hyde, in his novel, *Dr. Jekyll and Mr. Hyde*.

For some time Damien felt that he was catching leprosy because he was losing feeling in his left foot. In 1884 his superiors asked a doctor to examine him and he was officially diagnosed with leprosy. For the time being the illness remained a secret.

In 1885, Bishop Kockemann summoned Damien to Honolulu to have him examined by the bishop's own doctors. During the examination Damien realized to his horror that the doctors were looking for signs of syphilis, not leprosy, since it was still widely believed that leprosy came from syphilis. Rumors had circulated that Damien had not kept his vow of chastity and the doctors asked him direct questions about his sexual life. Damien replied that he had always strictly kept his vow, that he had never had relations with either a man or a woman. The doctors found no signs of syphilis.

In January 1885, while on retreat in Honolulu, Damien tried to relieve pain in his leg with a warm footbath. He put hot water in a basin and put his foot in. Soon he saw in the basin pieces of skin floating on the water. He had badly scalded his foot and hadn't felt it. He screamed and other priests came running. "I've scalded my foot," he said, "I'm a leper!"

The disease soon spread and Damien could no longer leave the leprosy settlement. His last time away was July 16, 1886.

Now Damien was anxious to get help as the disease spread. On July 29, 1886 Joseph Ira Dutton arrived. He was a Civil War veteran in the United States who wished to do penance for a sinful life by cutting himself off from the world. He proved to be a valuable assistant to Damien, although they sometimes had their disagreements.

Father Damien was particularly anxious to get nuns to come to staff the hospital. There were Franciscan nuns in the hospital in Honolulu who cared for those in the first stages of leprosy, but he couldn't convince them to come to Molokai. Forty more exiles were arriving every week and the death rate continued high. In March 1888 there were 749 leprosy victims in the settlement and eighty boys in the orphanage. Meanwhile, Damien's disease spread. His ears were protruding, the bridge of his nose had collapsed, and his right hand was covered with lepromas—except for the fingers that held the consecrated host when he celebrated Mass. He badly needed help. Finally, in 1888, three Franciscan nuns were sent to Molokai.

By now Damien's sores had begun to suppurate. His eyes were always inflamed, making it impossible for him to read, and he had breathing problems. Damien knew well that these symptoms meant that death was near. In his last letter to his brother Pamphile, on February 12, 1889, he said that he wished only that God's will should be done. He said that he now had more help for his thousand lepers and more than a hundred orphans: two priests, two brothers, and three sisters.

He died on Palm Sunday, April 15, 1889. After his death, all signs of leprosy disappeared from his face. He was buried in Molokai but in 1936 his body was returned to the Sacred Hearts Church in Leuven, Belgium.

Leprosy still exists in the world, although it can now be treated. The World Health Organization estimates that there are still fifteen million cases of leprosy, now usually called Hanson's Disease, almost all in Third World countries.

Pope John Paul II was scheduled to beatify Damien in May 1994, but he broke his hip a few days before. The ceremony took place on June 4, 1995.

CHAPTER 16

Saint Frances Xavier Cabrini

(*1850-1917*)

Of all the saints and blesseds in this book, Saint Frances Xavier Cabrini comes the closest to being *the* saint of the Americas. She established convents, academies, hospitals, and orphanages throughout the United States, but also in Central and South America—in Nicaragua, Panama, Argentina and Brazil. She didn't make it to Canada or Mexico, but she was active in more parts of the Americas than any other American saint was.

When she was canonized in 1946, she was the first citizen of the United States to receive that honor.

She was born Maria Francesca on July 15, 1850, at Sant' Angelo Lodigiano, between Pavia and Lodi in Lombardy, Italy. She was the youngest of the thirteen children of Agostino, a farmer, and Stella Oldini Cabrini. Her parents and siblings called her Cecchina as she was growing up. When she was thirteen, her sister Rosa, fifteen years older than she and a strict schoolteacher, began to take charge of her as her parents aged; they died when she was twenty. One of the periodicals in the home was the *Annals of the Propagation of the Faith* and from reading this Cecchina dreamed of becoming a missionary in China.

She received a teacher's license and began to teach when she was eighteen. When she was 22, she applied for admission to the religious community at whose school she had been, but she was denied because of her poor health. She tried another community, with the same result. She continued to teach but joined the Third Order of Saint Francis and spent some of her spare time visiting the poor and teaching catechism.

She had attracted the notice of a priest, Father Serrati, in whose school she was working. In 1874, he was appointed provost of the collegiate church at Codogno and found in his new parish a small orphanage that was being operated by its eccentric foundress, Sister Antonia Tondini, and two other women. Father Serrati thought that the orphanage was being mismanaged and asked Maria Francesca to join the staff and improve the situation. Reluctantly, she did so.

She and two of her pupils began wearing a religious habit like that worn by Sister Antonia and her companions. She also recruited several other women and in 1877 all seven of the women took their first vows. At the same time, Bishop Dominic Gelmini of Lodi appointed Maria Francesca the superior. This antagonized Sister Antonia, whose behavior became a scandal. The other sisters tried to persevere in their work, but finally the bishop gave up and suppressed both the orphanage and the convent. Bishop Gelmini told Sister Francesca, "You wanted to join a missionary sisterhood. With your seven companions you can now found one of your own."

With the bishop's blessing, Sister Francesca found a disused Franciscan friary in Codogno and the sisters moved in on November 14, 1880. She drew up a rule for the community and began to call herself Mother Francesca Saverio (Frances Xavier in English) Cabrini. The rule, approved by Bishop Gelmini, stipulated that the order, known as the Missionary Salesians of the Sacred Heart, would be primarily involved in the Christian education of girls. (In 1889 the name was changed to the Missionary Sisters of the Sacred Heart.)

It didn't take long for Mother Cabrini's community to start

expanding. Within two years another convent was established in Grumello and, in 1884, one in Milan. In 1887 she went to Rome to ask for the Holy See's approval of the rule for her community and for permission to open a house in Rome. She met with the Cardinal Vicar of Rome who told her that Rome had enough convents and to come back after her community had grown and developed further. Mother Cabrini simply asked the cardinal to show her rule to Pope Leo XIII. He did so and the pope not only approved the rule but also asked Mother Cabrini to open two houses in Rome, a free school and a children's home.

With her community established, Mother Cabrini still thought about becoming a missionary in China and taking her sisters there. However, the bishop of Piacenza had established the Society of Saint Charles in America to work with Italian immigrants and he suggested to Mother Cabrini that she go there to help with that work. Archbishop Michael Corrigan of New York even sent her an invitation. In 1888, Mother Cabrini had a private audience with Pope Leo XIII and she presented the matter to him. "Not to the East, but to the West," he told her. He convinced her that she was needed in America.

Of course, going to America meant sailing across the Atlantic Ocean, and that terrified Mother Cabrini. As a little girl she fell into a river and almost drowned, and from then on she had a fear of water. Nevertheless, she made arrangements for her and six other sisters to sail to New York. It turned out to be the first of 24 trans-Atlantic voyages she would take.

The seven sisters, along with 1,500 Italian immigrants, arrived in New York on March 31, 1889. They expected someone to be at the dock to meet them, but no one showed up and they spent the night in a shabby and verminous hotel near Chinatown. The next day they went to meet Archbishop Corrigan, who didn't exactly give them a warm welcome. "You might as well board the next ship and go back to Italy," he told them.

When he had invited the sisters to staff an orphanage, Archbishop Corrigan thought that the Countess Palma di Cesnola, whose maiden name had been Mary Reid, was going to contribute a building for that purpose. But when she rented a building on 59th Street, the archbishop didn't think it was suitable for an orphanage and the resulting disagreement between the countess and the archbishop ended with the countess withdrawing her offer. So the archbishop no longer had a place for the sisters.

When she was told that they might as well go back to Italy, Mother Cabrini replied, "The Holy Father has sent us, and we will stay!"

Seeing her determination, Archbishop Corrigan took them to the convent of the Sisters of Charity, across the street from his cathedral, and asked the superior there to give the Italian sisters food and shelter. After moving in, Mother Cabrini immediately went to work, begging money in order to open a day school. She also made friends with Countess Cesnola and reconciled her with the archbishop. Within a few weeks, Mother Cabrini found a house for her sisters and even made a start on an orphanage. Archbishop Corrigan celebrated the opening of the orphanage on May 3, 1889, only 34 days after the sisters' arrival in America.

In July letters arrived from Italy telling her about some difficulties that required her presence. She was, after all, still responsible for the religious community she founded in Italy. When she returned to Italy in July, she took with her two postulants for the order she had founded nine years earlier.

She remained in Italy for nine months before returning to New York in 1890. She spent 3½ months in New York, during which she acquired the former Jesuit novitiate at West Park in Ulster County. The orphanage was transferred there and this place became the American novitiate for the Missionary Sisters of the Sacred Heart.

Her third journey to Italy and back to New York was in 1891. This time she brought 29 sisters with her, making a total of fifty of Mother Cabrini's sisters in the United States. During this trip, she founded a small hospital, which later became New York's Columbus Hospital. Her community was growing, not only in the United States but also in Italy, where she began a new house near Rome and a students' hostel in Genoa.

In October 1891 Mother Cabrini and fourteen of her sisters sailed to Managua, Nicaragua, where they tried to open a school. These were revolutionary times in Central America, though, and the sisters were driven out. They moved to Panama. This was Mother Cabrini's first establishment in the Americas outside of the United States.

On her way back from Panama in 1892, she stopped in New Orleans at the request of Archbishop Francis Janssens and made a foundation there. Then she had to go back to Italy, where she remained for almost two years. During this time she continued her begging for all her foundations, including a request of Pope Leo XIII. He gave her $1,000 from his personal funds.

She was back in New York early in 1894, where she saw Columbus Hospital legally incorporated in the state of New York. Then she left for her first tour of South America, stopping on the way to visit her sisters in Panama. From there she sailed to Costa Rica, then on to Chile, crossed the Andes Mountains on the back of a mule, and continued on to Buenos Aires, Argentina. She opened an academy for girls there on March 1, 1896, the first of several houses she founded in Argentina. She would visit them again in 1900-1901 and 1908. On those trips she also founded houses in Brazil—in São Paulo in 1901 and Rio de Janeiro in 1908.

After that first foundation in Buenos Aires in 1896, Mother Cabrini again had to sail back to Italy to handle some serious problems. She had to cope with a long lawsuit in the ecclesiastical courts and she faced riots in Milan. She then traveled to other parts of Europe, making her first European foundations outside Italy in Paris, France. She was in England in 1898.

Then it was back to the United States again. In 1899 she led her community in taking over parochial schools in or near New York, Newark, Scranton, Chicago and Denver. She opened an orphanage in Arlington, New Jersey, and signed a deed for a boarding school in New York that was named Mother Cabrini High School.

Then it was back to Europe again. She established convents in Brockley, England; in and near Madrid, and at Bilbao, Spain.

She was in the United States for all of the years from 1902 to 1906, the longest uninterrupted period she spent here. It was a busy period indeed. She established convents, schools, orphanages, and hospitals in Chicago, Seattle and Los Angeles, and a "preventorium" for girls afflicted with tuberculosis in Burbank, California.

In Chicago she founded another Columbus Hospital in 1903. For that she bought the former North Shore Hotel fronting on Lincoln Park for $160,000, using $10,000 that she had begged for the down payment. The sellers tried to cheat her out of a strip of land 25 feet wide at the end of the property, but she measured the property herself. When she discovered dishonest contractors, she dismissed them and personally supervised the remodeling of the hotel into a hospital.

Mother Cabrini continued this schedule year after year. Perhaps the most amazing thing is that she was able to do it despite her poor health. She was, indeed, a frail, small, sickly woman who suffered from fevers that sometimes lasted for months, especially after she contracted malaria while in South America in 1908. At times she seemed to be completely exhausted. But it never slowed her down. "While I am at work," she said, "I am well. I fall sick the instant I stop working."

She also never permitted her activity and travels to interfere with her spiritual life. Indeed, they flowed from her zeal for the welfare of souls and her concern for the poor. She lived her life in continual prayer and intimate union with God.

The Vatican did not finally approve the constitutions for the Missionary Sisters of the Sacred Heart until 1907. By that time the order that began with eight members in 1880 had increased to more than a thousand. There were more than fifty foundations (and they would increase to 67 before her death)—schools, hospitals, orphanages, and other establishments. They were located in eight countries in Europe and the Americas. Mother Cabrini, though, denied that she had done any of it. "I have not done it," she said. "God has done it all, and I have merely looked on."

In 1909 Mother Cabrini did something that she had hoped to do earlier but never had sufficient time to do: While in Seattle she became a citizen of the United States.

She left Europe for the last time in 1912, two years before the First World War broke out in Europe. She continued to crisscross the United States—in Seattle to procure a place for an orphanage in 1913, and then back to New York to establish another orphanage at Dobb's Ferry; then in 1915 back to Seattle again where she acquired the Perry Hotel, which eventually became the St. Frances Cabrini Hospital. Then she went down to Los Angeles and from there to Chicago. She arrived at Columbus Hospital in Chicago on April 18, 1917. By this time it was apparent that her health was failing alarmingly.

She lived for another eight months, dying in the convent of the Columbus Hospital in Chicago on December 22, 1917. She was 67. After her funeral in Chicago, her body was interred at West Park in New York. In 1932 it was transferred to Mother Cabrini High School in Manhattan.

Pope Pius XI beatified her on November 13, 1938. Cardinal Mundelein of Chicago was present for the ceremony and gave the sermon. Part of that sermon sums up the life of Mother Cabrini as well as anything. He said: "When we contemplate this frail little woman, in the short space of two-score years, recruiting an army of four thousand women under the banner of the Sacred Heart of Jesus, dedicated to a life of poverty and self-sacrifice, fired by the enthusiasm of the Crusaders of old, burning with love of their fellowmen, crossing the seas, penetrating into unknown lands, teaching them and their children by word and example to become good Christians and law-abiding citizens, befriending the poor, teaching the ignorant, washing the sick, all without hope of reward or recompense here below—tell me, does not all this fulfill the concept of a noble woman?"

Pope Pius XII signed the decree of her canonization on January 11, 1944. However, since World War II was then in progress, the formal ceremony of canonization was delayed until 1946. Her feast is celebrated on November 13.

CHAPTER 17

Martyrs of Mexico

(1915-1937)

Perhaps it is fitting that Mexico, the country that produced the first saint of the Americas, Juan Diego, should also produce the most saints. Of the 137 American saints and blesseds, fifty are from Mexico. Of those fifty, all but six were martyrs. Fifteen of them were martyred in Japan rather than in Mexico and are mentioned briefly in the final chapter, as are three other blesseds who were martyred. This chapter is about the 26 men who were martyred in Mexico in the twentieth century.

The first of the martyrs to receive the honors of the Church was Miguel Agustín Pro, whom Pope John Paul II beatified September 25, 1988. The same pope canonized the other 25 on May 21, 2000. As this book was being prepared, it is expected that the pope will announce a date soon for the canonization of Miguel Pro.

First a little background is necessary. A revolution in 1910 brought a Socialist and anti-religion government into power. After two other men held the presidency, Venustiano Carranza made himself president. He called a Constitutional Convention in 1917 that adopted a constitution under which the state controlled religious worship.

Carranza was assassinated in 1920 and was succeeded by

General Alvaro Obregón, who in turn was followed by Plutarco Elías Calles. When Calles began to enforce the anti-religious laws with severity, Pope Pius XI wrote to the Mexican bishops in 1926 lamenting the hostile laws. After the government tried to make the Church a dependency of the state, the Mexican bishops issued a joint pastoral stating: "Further concession by us is not possible. It would be criminal to tolerate this situation any longer." The bishops suspended all public Masses and sacraments for three years, hoping that this step would increase opposition to the government from the predominantly Catholic population.

A petition to the government, signed by two million Mexican citizens, was ignored. Violence followed. Nearly 150 priests and civilians were killed and an armed rebellion, known as the Revolt of the *Cristeros*, broke out. Some of those killed are the martyrs who have been beatified and/or canonized.

Father Miguel Agustín Pro was born in 1891 and joined the Society of Jesus in 1911. Because of the persecution of the Church at that time, he was forced to leave Mexico in 1914. He resumed his studies in California and then in seminaries in Nicaragua, Spain and Belgium, where he was ordained to the priesthood in 1925. A year later he returned to Mexico to minister to the Catholic people despite government prohibition. He immediately founded a secret pastoral network, taking the Eucharist from house to house, organizing spiritual exercises for workers and students, and visiting prisoners. He also became a member of the National League for the Defense of Religious Liberty, which opposed the government's crackdown on the Catholic Church.

On November 13, 1927, a paramilitary wing of the National League for the Defense of Religious Liberty tried to assassinate former President and President-elect Obregón. As he was driving through Mexico City's Chapultepec Park, dynamite was hurled at his car from a passing vehicle. The assassination attempt was unsuccessful, but police stopped the car used in the attempt and three men were captured. The car was traced to Father Pro's brother,

Humberto. During torture, one of the men arrested told police that the dynamite bombs used in the attempt had been made in a house rented by Humberto.

Humberto and Miguel were both arrested although there was nothing to indicate that Miguel was involved in the bombing. Nevertheless, they and two of the men who attempted the assassination were killed by a firing squad, without a trial, on November 23, 1927. As the order to fire was being given to the firing squad, Father Pro spread his arms wide in emulation of Christ's death on the cross and shouted, "Long live Christ the King," the battle cry of the *Cristeros* in their rebellion against the government.

The Church's investigation into the execution concluded that Father Pro had nothing to do with the assassination attempt but that he was killed "in hatred of the faith."

Blessed Miguel Pro's feast is celebrated on November 23.

The 25 martyrs who were canonized on May 21, 2000 included 22 priests and three laymen. Here are brief stories of each:

Father Luis Batis Sainz, Manuel Morales, Salvador Lara Puente, and **David Roldán Lara** were all executed together on August 15, 1926, the feast of the Assumption of Mary. Father Batis was the pastor of the parish of San Pedro Chalchihuites, in the Archdiocese of Durango, in which the three young men were parishioners.

Manuel Morales was 28 when he was shot. He was known to be a solid Christian, a faithful husband, and the loving father of three young sons. He was a hard worker, a devoted layman who was active in his parish, and he had a special devotion to the Eucharist.

Salvador Lara Puente was barely 21 when he was shot. He was a handsome young man, tall and strong, known for his fine treatment of everyone. He cared for his widowed mother and was a hard-working employee of a mining company.

David Roldán Lara, the first cousin of Salvador Lara Puente, was 24 when he was shot. His father died when he was small and he was known as a caring son to his mother. He showed an eagerness for the apostolate as a member of Catholic Action of Mexican Youth.

On August 14, 1926, about fifteen days after the Mexican bishops had suspended all public worship as a protest against the government's anti-religious laws, Father Batis was taken prisoner. As he was being arrested, he said to the soldiers, "If it is the will of God, I will be one of the martyrs of the Church."

The following day, Manuel, Salvador and David learned about their pastor's arrest and they made plans to go to plead for his release. As soon as the group of young men met to decide what to do, a group of soldiers arrived and the chief shouted, "Manuel Morales!"

Manuel stepped forward and with grace replied, "I am he, at your orders."

The soldiers began to beat him furiously. While Salvador and David were retained, Manuel and Father Batis were led away to a place known as the "door of Saint Teresa." Father Batis pleaded with the soldiers to spare Manuel because he had a wife and children. Manuel spoke up and said to Father Batis, "I will die, but God does not die. He will care for my wife and my sons." Then he exclaimed, "Long live Christ the King and the Virgin of Guadalupe!"

Father Batis absolved his companion and said to him, "Until heaven." Seconds later both men suffered martyrdom.

It was then Salvador's and David's turn, a few meters away. Salvador walked, smiling as usual, while praying in a low voice. David remained serene as he walked with his cousin to the appointed place. They faced the firing squad, and died bravely.

Father David Galván Bermúdez was the first of the martyrs to die, on January 30, 1915. He was ministering spiritually to wounded soldiers in Guadalajara when he was taken prisoner. After his execution his companion in prison commented that Father Galván had calmly told him, "Today we are going to go to eat with God." As he stood in front of the firing squad, he pointed to his chest to show the soldiers where to aim.

Father Cristóbal Magallanes Jara was pastor in Totatiche, Jalisco, where he was known as a zealous priest, a prudent mentor for his fellow priests, an ardent promoter of the rosary, and active in the promotion of the human and Christian rights of his parishioners. When the persecutors of the Church closed the Seminary of Guadalajara, he offered to fund in his parish a seminary to form future priests. He was arrested with Father Agustín Caloca and he tried to comfort the younger priest, saying, "Courage, son, only a moment and then heaven." Later, confronting the soldiers, he exclaimed, "I die innocent, and I pray to God that my blood will serve the unity of my Mexican brethren." He was shot May 25, 1927.

Father Agustín Caloca Cortés was martyred with Father Magallanes. Father Caloca was serving as the prefect in the seminary established by the older priest. As he stood in front of the platoon in charge of his execution, he was encouraged by the words of Father Magallanes and exclaimed, "For God we live and for him we die."

Father Jenaro Sánchez Delgadillo was vicar of the parish in Tecolotlan, Jalisco. He was taken prisoner along with some parishioners. The others were freed, but Father Sánchez was taken to a tree prepared as a gallows. With heroic serenity, Father Sánchez said, "Good friends, they are going to hang me. I forgive them, that my God also will forgive them, and long live Christ the King." The executioners pulled the rope with such force that his head hit the branch of the tree with great force. He died January 17, 1927.

Father Jesús Méndez Montoya was taken prisoner on February 5, 1928 after federal troops forced a small group of Christians to lead them to the place where he was hiding. As the troops arrived, Father Méndez tried to save some consecrated hosts, asking the soldiers for a moment so he could consume the Blessed Sacrament. They allowed it. Then with meekness he turned to his sisters and said, "It is God's will." The soldiers took him a few meters outside the patio of the church and killed him with three shots.

Father José Isabel Flores Varela was chaplain of a parish in

Zapotlenejo, Jalasco. An old companion whom Father Flores had protected denounced him before the political boss of Zapotlenejo and he was apprehended on June 18, 1927 while he was on his way to a group of huts to celebrate the Eucharist. He was imprisoned in a filthy room, tied and maltreated. On June 21, he was conducted, at night, to the cemetery with the intention of hanging him there, but they could not. The chief ordered him to be shot, but a soldier who recognized the priest as the one who had baptized him refused to do it. At that, the executioner murdered the soldier. Then, mysteriously, the weapons of the other soldiers could not fire. Finally, one of the soldiers slashed Father Flores' throat with a large knife.

Father José María Robles Hurtado was pastor of Tecolotlan, Jalasco, and founder of the religious congregation Sisters of the Sacred Heart of Jesus. He was hanged on an oak tree on June 26, 1927.

Father Julio Alvarez Mendoza passed his entire priestly life in the parish at Mechoacanejo, Jalasco. As he was on his way to a ranch to minister to the people there, he was recognized as a priest and apprehended by members of the army. On March 30, 1927, as he was placed on a pile of garbage, he said softly, "I am going to die innocent. I have not done anything bad. My crime is to be a minister of God. I forgive you." He crossed his arms and awaited the bullets.

Father David Uribe Velasco was pastor of a parish in Iguala of the Diocese of Chilapa. He ministered among masons, Protestants and a group of schismatics. The military arrested him and proposed to grant him his freedom if he would agree to be bishop of the schismatic church created by the government. Father Uribe refused and wrote a defense of his faith. He wrote: "If I was consecrated with the holy oil that has made me a minister of the Almighty, why not be consecrated with my blood in defense of the souls redeemed with the blood of Christ? ... What joy to die in defense of the rights of God!"

While in prison he wrote his last words: "I declare that I am innocent of the crimes that I am accused of.... I am in the hands of God and of the Virgin of Guadalupe. I ask pardon of God and pardon of my enemies; I ask pardon of those whom I have offended." He was shot in the nape of the neck on April 12, 1927.

Father Margarito Flores García was a priest only three years when he read the last words of Father Uribe and of his heroic death. He exclaimed, "I too am going to give my life for Christ. I am going to ask permission of my superior and I am going to undertake the fullness of martyrdom." His time came on November 12, 1927, when he was ordered before a firing squad.

Father Pedro Esqueda Ramírez had as his greatest passion the religious education of children. He founded various centers of study and a school for the formation of catechists. After his arrest, he was taken on November 22, 1927 from his prison to the place of execution. Children surrounded him and Father Esqueda repeated to those who walked with him: "Do not stop studying your catechism, do not abandon Christian doctrine for anything." On a small piece of paper he wrote his final recommendations for the catechists. He was killed with three shots.

Father Rodrigo Aguilar Alemán was pastor of Union de Jula, Jalasco. At dawn on October 28, 1927 he was taken to a plaza to be hanged from a mango tree. To test his fortitude, his executioners placed the rope around his neck and arrogantly asked him, "Who lives?" He valiantly responded, "Christ the King and Saint Mary of Guadalupe!" The soldiers pulled the rope with enough force to raise him from the ground. They lowered him again and repeated the question, "Who lives?" For the second time, Father Aguilar said in a firm voice, "Christ the King and Saint Mary of Guadalupe!" He was again pulled from the ground and then lowered and a third time was asked, "Who lives?" With his last breath, he repeated again, "Christ the King and Saint Mary of Guadalupe."

Father Román Adame Rosales continued to administer the sacraments during the persecution. He was betrayed and taken prisoner. On April 21, 1927, as he was taken to the place of execution, he tried unsuccessfully to save the life of a soldier who did not want to shoot the priest and was therefore shot himself. Then, resolved and firm, but humbly, the priest gave up his life.

Father Sabas Reyes Salazar was arrested during Holy Week of 1927. Federal troops were searching for Father Francisco Vizcarra and his ministers, but found only Father Reyes, on whom they concentrated their hatred. They tied him to a column in the church and tortured him for three days, denying him food and water and burning his hands. On April 13, 1927 they took him to the cemetery where they shot him while he exclaimed, "Long live Christ the King!"

Father Toribio Romo González had been working all day and all night on Friday, February 24, 1928. At 5 a.m. on Saturday, he wanted to celebrate the Eucharist but, feeling very tired, decided to sleep awhile in order to celebrate better. He had scarcely fallen asleep when a group of soldiers entered the room. When one of them said to the others, "That is the priest, kill him," Father Romo awakened, sat up and receive a bullet from a gun. Wounded, he tried to get up but another shot ended his life.

Father Tranquilino Ubiarco Robles was preparing to celebrate the Eucharist and bless a marriage when he was taken prisoner and condemned to death by hanging from a tree in a park in Tepatitlan, Jalasco. As he was being hanged at dawn on October 5, 1928, he repeated the words of Christ, "Today you will be with me in paradise."

Father Justino Orona Madrigal was with his vicar, Father Atilóno Cruz. One night they were sleeping in a house at the Las Cruces ranch, near Cuquio. At dawn on July 1, 1928 federal forces and the municipal president of Cuquio arrived at the ranch and beat on the door where the priests were sleeping. Father Orona opened the door and with a strong voice greeted his executioners with, "Long live Christ the King!" The response was a shower of bullets.

Father Atilóno Cruz Alvarado was asleep with Father Orona when the soldiers arrived. When he heard the shots that killed his superior, he knelt in his bed and awaited the moment of his own sacrifice. He was riddled with bullets.

Father Mateo Correa Magallanes, who had been pursued continually, was finally apprehended when he was visiting a sick person in Fresnillo, Zacatecas. He was threatened with death if he did not reveal what he had heard in confession. He replied with dignity, "You can do it, but you know that a priest must keep the secret of confession. I am willing to die." He was shot on February 6, 1927.

Father Miguel de la Mora was chaplain of the cathedral in Colima, the first city in the Mexican Republic to require the registration of priests in order to grant them licenses to practice. The bishop and his priests protested and affirmed their fidelity to the faith. The governor responded by exiling all the priests. Father Miguel and some others hid in order to continue to give help to the faithful. He was discovered and threatened with jail if he did not resume worship in the cathedral against the orders of the bishop. With the pressure of the governor, he said that he preferred to leave the city. On the way, he was apprehended and taken to the general, who condemned him to be shot. He walked in silence until he reached the place indicated and there proclaimed his faith and his love for Mary. He pulled out his rosary and began to pray. With the rosary in his hand, he received the bullets on August 7, 1927.

Father Pedro de Jesús Maldonado Lucero, pastor of Santa Isabel in Chihuahua, was the last of the martyrs to die, ten years after most of the other. He was known for his devotion to the Blessed Sacrament. On the Wednesday of Holy Week in 1937, a group of armed men confronted him while he was carrying a ciborium with consecrated hosts. They struck him with a pistol, fracturing his skull above his left eye. He was washed in blood and almost unconscious. The ciborium was opened and the hosts thrown away. However, one of the soldiers gave him a host and said, "Eat this." The priest did so. He was taken to a hospital where he died the following day, Holy Thursday, the anniversary of his priestly ordination.

CHAPTER 18

Blessed André Bessette

(1845-1937)

One of the most impressive sights in Montreal, Quebec, Canada is the magnificent Saint Joseph's Oratory at the top of Mount Royal, overlooking the city. The basilica is one of the largest ecclesiastical buildings in the world and thousands of people visit it every year to pray to Saint Joseph of Nazareth, the foster-father of Jesus. This splendid church owes its existence to the efforts of a small, humble brother known to the world as Brother André of the Congregation of Holy Cross. His story shows what a sickly man with a poor education could accomplish because of his faith in God and in Saint Joseph.

Brother André was also known as "the Miracle Man of Montreal," the name of the first biography written about him. During his lifetime, though, nothing made Brother André angrier than to have someone say that he performed miracles. He always insisted that it was Saint Joseph, not he, who cured people.

André Bessette was born on August 9, 1845, the eighth of Isaac and Clothilde Foisy Bessette's twelve children, in the small village of St.-Gregoire d'Iberville, near Montreal. He was born with a severe stomach ailment and was considered to be so ill that the midwife baptized him immediately. He was given the name Alfred.

His parents were poor and the older children helped by finding odd jobs in the village or assisting their father with wood-cutting in the forest that surrounded their home. Alfred, though, could not help because he was too weak. He could not eat solid foods because of his stomach problems and his mother had to prepare foods that he could digest.

In 1855, when Alfred was nine, tragedy struck the family when Isaac was killed while he was cutting wood. A large tree fell on him and crushed him to death. Afterward, his mother tried to keep the family together but then she contracted tuberculosis and had to find other homes for her children. She kept only Alfred with her because he was so ill. They moved to St.-Cesaire to live with Clothilde's sister Mary and her husband, Timothe Nadeau. Clothilde died in 1857 when she was 43 and Alfred eleven.

Because they had to be so close, his mother's death was particularly hard for Alfred. However, he had the consolation of his faith. His mother had been a devout woman who passed on to Alfred her devotion to Saint Joseph. Alfred also liked to assist at Mass in the parish church and became a friend of the pastor, Father André Provençal.

Alfred continued to live with the Nadeau family after his mother's death. He tried to do his share of the work, but he was simply too weak to do manual labor. His uncle Timothe, a robust and energetic man, was not sympathetic and nagged Alfred constantly. Alfred tried shoe-making but that, too, was too hard for his limited strength. When Louis Ouimet, mayor of St.-Cesaire, took an interest in Alfred and offered to adopt him, Timothe and Mary readily agreed, and the fifteen-year-old moved to the Ouimet farm. After a year at the farm, he tried several other jobs—a baker in the village bakery, a tinsmith and a blacksmith—but failed at all three trades because of his poor health.

The end of the Civil War in the United States had brought prosperity to the industries of New England, so as Alfred reached his late teens he joined other French Canadians migrating to the United States to work in factories. He ended up in Connecticut.

His poor health continued to plague him and he constantly had to search for light work. One benefit of the four years he worked in the United States was that he learned to speak English. He returned to St.-Cesaire in 1867.

Shortly after his return, Father Provençal introduced him to the Holy Cross Brothers. The Congregation of Holy Cross had been founded in France by Father Basil Moreau and had come to Canada in 1847. Father Provençal was convinced that Alfred belonged in religious life, but Alfred wasn't so sure.

"But Father," he said when the priest suggested that he should be a brother of Holy Cross, "I can neither read nor write!"

Father Provençal replied, "You do not need to know how to read and write, young man, to pray."

Alfred spent the next few years in indecision but, in 1870, when he was 25, he entered Notre Dame College, the Holy Cross novitiate and school in Montreal. Father Provençal sent a letter along to Father Julien Gastineau, principal of the school and master of novices, that said, "I am sending you a saint."

In December 1870, when he received his first religious habit, Alfred changed his name to André in honor of Father André Provençal.

During his novitiate year in the congregation, André was assigned to the laundry and linen supply for the novitiate and school. He also mopped corridors, tended the infirmary, and did whatever anyone asked him to do. André was happier than he had been since before his mother died, and he looked forward to being a Holy Cross brother.

That almost didn't happen. At the end of his novitiate year, his superiors decided not to allow André to profess his vows. It was up to the novice master to break the news to him. He told him, "Brother, I must advise you, the superiors have voted not to admit you to our congregation at this time. Our decision is based on the fact that your health is so delicate. You know, I am sure, that once the congregation accepts you as a professed member, it is responsible for you in sickness and in health. Our experience during the past year leads us to believe your health would not survive the rigors of our life."

André replied simply, "I accept the judgment as the will of God. I must add that I have been deeply happy as a novice, happier than I have been in my whole life."

The superiors agreed, however, to give André a six-month extension of his novitiate, hoping that his health might improve. André knew that it wouldn't, but he accepted the six months.

A few days later, Bishop Ignace Bourget of Montreal visited Notre Dame College. André asked for the opportunity to speak with him privately and, when it was granted, asked the bishop to help him become a brother. Bishop Bourget replied, "Do not fear, my dear son, you will be allowed to make your religious profession."

With both the bishop and the novice master pleading his case, the council reluctantly agreed to permit André to profess the vows of the congregation, and he did so on August 22, 1872.

For the next forty years, Brother André served as porter of Notre Dame College, greeting all those who entered. In his later years, he joked, "When I joined the community, the superiors showed me the door and I remained there for forty years."

His small room near the door held a narrow wooden couch, a crucifix on the wall, and a small statue of Saint Joseph on the windowsill. The window looked out on Mount Royal and Brother André turned the statue so that it faced the mountain. When he was asked why he did that, he replied, "Because some day Saint Joseph is going to be honored in a very special way on Mount Royal."

Brother André had other duties besides porter. He continued to work in the laundry and did sacristan work. He also performed messenger services, taking messages to people in town or going to the Post Office. Sometimes, while on his errands, he would hear about someone who was ill and he made it a practice to visit the person to cheer him or her up and to pray with him or her. He would also rub the sick person with a little oil taken from a vigil lamp burning in front of Saint Joseph's statue in the college's chapel.

Soon after Brother André began to visit the sick and rub them with Saint Joseph's oil, it became evident that cures were taking place. People began to search out Brother André to visit their sick relatives and friends. At first only a few came but soon ill people were crowding the corridors of the school and the chapel. André would stand patiently as each visitor described his or her ailment. Then he would say something to console them and either rub some of Saint Joseph's oil on them or touch them with a medal of Saint Joseph. Cures were frequent and sometimes spontaneous.

The number of visitors at the college to see Brother André became disruptive, to say the least. His superiors didn't want to turn the people away, so they asked him to meet the visitors at a small trolley station across the street from the college. André obeyed, but then trolley passengers began to complain about the presence of contagiously ill people in the trolley station. The ill people also continued to go to the college.

Brother André was now controversial. Medical doctors charged him with quackery and religious authorities accused him of superstition because of the use of the oil. The more people called him a miracle worker the more André insisted, over and over again, "I do not cure. Saint Joseph cures." The adulation and the controversy that surrounded him distressed André. Finally, Saint Joseph came to the rescue.

The Holy Cross authorities had been trying to buy land on Mount Royal, but unsuccessfully. Brother André and others began to plant Saint Joseph medals on the property and, in 1896, when Brother André was 51, the owners finally agreed to sell the property. André then went to his superiors and asked for permission to build a small oratory in honor of Saint Joseph on the mountain. He told them that he could then receive the sick there. The superiors didn't grant the full request, but allowed André to place a statue of Saint Joseph in a small niche on the mountain and to raise money for a future project in honor of Saint Joseph.

In 1904, eight years after the congregation bought the property, André was given permission to construct a small chapel on the mountain. Now sixty years old, André supervised the project with great zeal. It was not a large chapel, only large enough to accommodate an altar, a priest and altar servers. But it was a start.

Since it was so small and provided no shelter, it did not solve the problem of keeping sick people away from the college. So in 1908, a group of laymen organized to enlarge the chapel. When completed, it could hold 200 people in all kinds of weather. A religious article shop, a restaurant, an office for André, and a waiting room for the sick were added. Brother André was released from his assignment as porter at the college and appointed guardian of the shrine. He took up residence at the new oratory.

Pilgrims began to come by the thousands and André spent eight to ten hours a day in his new office, receiving thirty to forty people an hour. Cured people left crutches, canes, and braces behind when they no longer needed them. In 1916, 435 cures were recorded. After he met with the sick, André took care of his mail, more than 80,000 letters a year that he received, requiring four secretaries to answer them. Then he often went into Montreal to visit the sick before returning to the oratory to spend most of the night in prayer.

Brother André, however, was not satisfied with his oratory. He wanted to build a shrine to Saint Joseph so great that it would attract the attention of all those who visited Montreal. As World War I started, he began to raise the money required to build his shrine, and he spent the next two decades doing so. Slowly work on the shrine began, first the crypt and then the gleaming white walls. In 1931, though, work stopped because the money ran out. Brother André, now in his eighties, stepped up his fund-raising efforts with several visits to the United States and throughout Canada.

In 1936, in the middle of the Depression, the Holy Cross authorities called a meeting to decide whether to complete the shrine or abandon it. André, now 91, was called into the meeting. He told his superiors, "Put a statue of Saint Joseph in the middle of the building. If he wants a roof over his head, he'll get it." The

Holy Cross authorities did exactly what Brother André recommended and within two months they had enough money to resume construction.

Brother André was always aware of the fact that he would not live to see the completion of the basilica. That didn't bother him because he knew that the work would be done. "It's not my project anyway," he insisted. "It's Saint Joseph's."

The upper church of the basilica was not completely finished until 1967—thirty years after Brother André's death. When completed Saint Joseph's Oratory rose 506 feet above street level, the highest point in Montreal.

In late December 1936, Brother André suffered an attack of acute gastritis and shortly after the New Year in 1937 he had a stroke. He lapsed into a coma and died on January 6, 1937. The sickly boy and weak youth reached the age of 91, outliving most of his contemporaries. More than a million people passed by his coffin as he lay in state before his burial. He was buried in a simple tomb in the basilica that he helped Saint Joseph to build.

Pope John Paul II beatified Brother André on May 23, 1982. His feast is celebrated on January 6.

CHAPTER 19

Saint Katharine Drexel

(1858-1955)

As this book is being published, Katharine Mary Drexel is the most recent person in the Americas to be canonized. She is also the only born citizen of the United States to be beatified or canonized. Kateri Tekakwitha and Elizabeth Ann Seton are the only others who were born in what is now the United States and they were both born before the United States was a separate country.

"Miss Drexel Enters a Catholic Convent" the headline read in *The Philadelphia Public Ledger*. "Gives Up Seven Million," said the subhead. This news indicates how prominent Katharine Drexel and her sisters were in Philadelphia society in the 1880's, and the surprise the newspaper's editors felt that someone would give up a fortune in order to become a nun.

Katharine did indeed inherit a large fortune—much larger in the late nineteenth century than the same amount would be today. She didn't entirely give up the fortune, though. She used it to help the poorest people in American society, the blacks (usually called Negroes or Coloreds in those days) and the Indians. She entered a convent to prepare herself to found an institute devoted entirely to helping them.

Katharine was born on November 26, 1858, the second

daughter of Francis Drexel and Hannah Langstroth, a Philadelphia Baptist-Quaker. Francis and his two brothers ran an international banking empire in partnership with J.P. Morgan in New York and the House of Morgan in London. The Drexels were among the wealthiest families in the United States. Katharine's older sister, Elizabeth, was born three years earlier.

Hannah died five weeks after Katharine's birth and for two years Francis' brother Anthony and his wife cared for Katharine and Elizabeth. In 1860 Francis married Emma Bouvier, the daughter of another prestigious Philadelphia family, and they had a daughter, Louise, in 1863.

Emma was a loving mother to her two stepchildren and she shared her husband's spiritual nature and generous spirit. The three girls knew that their father, as busy as he was making money in the banking business, also spent a half-hour each evening in prayer and that he insisted on helping the poor in every way he could. Emma was in charge of making the financial contributions for the family, which she did prudently and skillfully. She also opened their home to the poor three days a week and the three girls helped their mother serve the poor. Emma also began a Sunday school for the children of employees and neighbors and, when they were old enough, the Drexel girls taught the children.

In 1870 Francis purchased a great estate in Torresdale, Pennsylvania, known as Saint Michel, that became their summer home. The grounds included sloping lawns, flower gardens and stately trees.

Francis and Emma hired tutors to give the three girls as fine an education as possible. Their education included extensive travel, especially in Europe. Katharine made her debut into Philadelphia society when she was twenty.

Father James O'Connor, the pastor at the church the Drexels usually attended, became a good friend of the family and Katharine's spiritual director. When Katharine confided in him that her life in the wealthy society gave her a feeling of dissatisfaction and that she felt a call to religious life, Father O'Connor counseled her to wait and pray.

Then Father O'Connor was named Bishop of Omaha, Nebraska. Communication between him and Katharine continued through extensive correspondence.

Late in 1879, when Katharine was 21, her stepmother developed cancer and suffered greatly for three years. While Katharine nursed her, she saw clearly that all the Drexel money couldn't spare her mother from suffering and she questioned the meaning of wealth, power and prestige. However, when she wrote to Bishop O'Connor for advice, he still replied, "Think, pray, and wait."

After their mother's death on January 29, 1883, Francis took the three young Drexel women on an extensive European tour to lighten their grief. They didn't return home until May of 1884. Then, five months later, the family went on a business trip to the Pacific Northwest, traveling in a plush private railroad car called "The Yellowstone," provided by the Northern Pacific Railroad.

On a quiet Sunday afternoon in February of 1885, while reading a book, Francis suddenly slumped forward and died. His will bequeathed one-tenth of his estate for immediate distribution to charities with the remainder to go into a trust fund, with each of his three daughters receiving one-third of the fund's annual net income. Newspapers reported that the sisters would each receive about 1,000 dollars a day.

Shortly after Francis' death, two missionaries arrived at the Drexel home seeking financial assistance. They were Benedictine Bishop Martin Marty, vicar apostolic of Dakota, and Father Joseph Stephan, director of the Bureau of Catholic Indian Missions. Katharine already had an interest in the evangelization of the Indians and she had recently read the book *A Century of Dishonor*, by Helen Hunt Jackson, that described the disgraceful history of Indian-white relations in the United States. The Drexel women promised to help the two missionaries.

At that time, though, Katharine's health was not good. The deaths of both parents within two years had taken their toll. She had lost weight and her usual vitality. Doctors suggested that she go to the Schwalbach Baths in Germany for treatment. Elizabeth and Louise went with her in 1886 and Katharine's health gradually improved.

While in Europe, the sisters tried to recruit priests and nuns for the Indian missions in the United States. In January of 1887 they had an audience with Pope Leo XIII and Katharine asked him to send more missionaries to the Indians. He replied, "Why don't *you* become a missionary?" The response took her by surprise. Although she had long considered becoming a nun, she had thought of the contemplative life.

After returning to the United States, the three Drexel women accepted Father Stephan's invitation to visit Indian missions in the Dakotas. They met Bishop O'Connor in Omaha and traveled by horseback, wagon and railroad to the Dakotas. Father Stephan showed her conditions in the Indian missions that Katharine never imagined existed, despite all she had read. The priest also introduced them to the famous Sioux chief Red Cloud and told him that the sisters were going to provide a school for the education of the tribe's children. Red Cloud never forgot the sisters' generosity.

Thus began Katharine's systematic financial aid to the Indian missions. Within four years, she financed the construction and support of thirteen mission schools stretching from the Dakotas through Wyoming and Montana to California and Oregon, and then down to New Mexico. This aid was to continue so that, in twenty years, the Drexel sisters contributed a million and a half dollars toward Indian Catholic education.

Katharine, though, was not satisfied to give only financial support. She still felt the call to religious life, but whenever she mentioned it to Bishop O'Connor he continued to tell her to wait. However, in 1889, as her sister Louise was preparing to marry Edward Morell, a prominent lawyer, Katharine wrote to Bishop O'Connor, "I am not obliged to submit my judgment to yours."

Bishop O'Connor then wrote to her, "You have decided to become a religious. The next thing for you to determine is whether you shall establish a new order for the Indian and Colored people."

That was not at all what Katharine had in mind, and she told

Bishop O'Connor that in several other letters. The bishop at first responded, "It's all right, Kate; it's like an invitation to a wedding. You don't have to take it if you don't want to." But soon the bishop became ever more insistent until it reached the point that he said that it was no longer "an open question" or an invitation; it was an order.

Katharine capitulated. On March 19, 1889 she wrote to Bishop O'Connor: "The feast of Saint Joseph brought me the grace to give the remainder of my life to the Indians and Coloreds, to enter fully and entirely into your view as to what is best for the salvation of the souls of these people."

Once Katharine's mind was made up, Bishop O'Connor asked the Sisters of Mercy in Pittsburgh to train her for religious life. It was when she entered that convent as a postulant on May 7, 1889 that the newspapers shouted that a Drexel sister had given up seven million dollars. Katharine was thirty years old. On November 7, 1889 she received the religious habit and the name Sister Mary Katharine.

Three important events occurred in 1890: In January, Katharine's sister Elizabeth married Walter George Smith, another prominent lawyer. Katharine was delighted that both of her sisters were now married. In May, Bishop O'Connor died in Omaha. This was a blow to Katharine, who had relied so heavily on the bishop. She believed that his death meant that the founding of a new order was not God's will. But Philadelphia's Archbishop Patrick J. Ryan wrote a note of sympathy to Katharine and then visited her. After listening quietly to her fears about the foundation of a new order, he asked simply, "If I share the burden with you, if I help you, can you go on?" Archbishop Ryan now became her spiritual guide.

The third important event in 1890, late in September, was Elizabeth's death after giving birth to a premature child, who also died. Within four years, Katharine had lost her stepmother, her father, Bishop O'Connor, and her older sister.

Katharine professed her vows as the first Sister of the Blessed

Sacrament for Indians and Colored People on February 12, 1891. Archbishop Ryan received her vows and invested her with the black veil. Besides the vows of poverty, chastity and obedience, Katharine added a fourth: "to be the mother and servant of the Indian and Negro races."

During her novitiate, Katharine had purchased a sixty-acre site in Cornwell Heights (now Bensalem), Pennsylvania, and began construction of her new order's motherhouse. The building wasn't finished yet when she professed her vows, so she and thirteen companions (ten novices and three postulants) moved into the Drexel summer home, St. Michel, in Torresdale. By the end of 1891 the community had 21 members.

Mother Katharine was to direct her community for the next 44 years.

The sisters moved into Saint Elizabeth's Convent (named for her sister) in 1892, even though construction wasn't yet finished. They took with them the pupils of Holy Providence School, a boarding school for poor children that Mother Katharine had already founded in Torresdale.

Archbishop Ryan was true to his word of helping Mother Katharine. Despite the sisters' eagerness to begin their missionary work, he did not permit them to leave Saint Elizabeth's Convent until they completed 3½ years of training. Their first effort was a boarding school at Saint Catherine's Mission in Santa Fe, New Mexico.

Mother Katharine's concern for poor black people paralleled her concern for Indians. She founded Saint Francis Industrial School (named after her father) in Eddington, Pennsylvania, where orphan boys, black and white, could learn a trade; it was Pennsylvania's first trade school. In 1894 she established Saint Emma's Industrial and Agricultural Institute (named after her stepmother) for young black men on the James River forty miles northwest of Richmond, Virginia. Then she purchased adjoining property and built a school for black girls, naming it Saint Francis de Sales, again after her father.

She constantly met opposition from anti-black white people. The barn at Saint Francis School was burned and other places were sometimes vandalized. Katharine continued her efforts undaunted.

Mother Katharine traveled throughout the southern United States looking for opportunities for her sisters to serve black people, and she visited the missions in the southwestern United States serving the Indians. She opened both boarding and day schools in the East, Midwest, South and Southwest. By 1942, she had established a system of black Catholic schools in thirteen states, with thirty convents, forty mission centers and 23 rural schools in which 15,000 children came under the care of the Sisters of the Blessed Sacrament. At the same time, she established fifty missions for Indians in sixteen states.

While supervising all this missionary activity, Mother Katharine still had to put her new order on a firm footing, which, among other things, meant writing a rule for the order. Two saints met when Mother Frances Xavier Cabrini advised Mother Katharine that the best way to get the rule approved was to personally take it to Rome. Mother Katharine left for Rome in May of 1907 and remained there until Pope Pius X gave preliminary approval the following July. When she returned, Archbishop Ryan conducted the order's first elections and, of course, the community elected Mother Katharine superior general. With the rule approved, the community branched out, opening new missions in Boston, New York, Chicago, Columbus, and Cincinnati.

In 1912, while visiting missions in New Mexico, Mother Katharine became seriously ill from typhoid fever complicated by bronchial pneumonia, a heart dysfunction, and nervous exhaustion. She returned to Pennsylvania and entered the infirmary at the motherhouse. By January she was well enough to sail for Rome again to complete negotiations for final approval of her rule.

One of Mother Katharine's great achievements was the founding of Xavier University in New Orleans, the first U.S. Catholic institution of higher learning for blacks. In 1925 Xavier received its charter as a college of liberal arts and sciences. By 1932, it reached university status and in 1934 four graduate schools were in operation.

In 1935, when she was 77, Mother Katharine suffered a severe heart attack during an extensive visitation of missions in the West. Doctors urged her to retire, so she relinquished control of her community after directing it for 44 years. She moved into the infirmary at Cornwell Heights. But her life was not yet over. For almost twenty more years she spent her days in constant prayer in a small room overlooking the sanctuary of the chapel. She never interfered with her successors' direction of the order. She had at last achieved her desire to be a contemplative nun.

She died peacefully on March 3, 1955. Pope John Paul II beatified her on November 20, 1988 and the same pope canonized her on October 1, 2000. Her feast is celebrated on March 3.

Chapter 20

Other American Saints and Blesseds

Holy men and women from fourteen countries on the American continents have been beatified or canonized. We have met 55 of them in the previous nineteen chapters. In this chapter, unfortunately, we can give only brief profiles to those not included in the earlier chapters.

Both Canada and the United States can rightly claim the eight Jesuit North American martyrs portrayed in Chapter 4 and Blessed Kateri Tekakwitha, profiled in Chapter 5. Canada has two other saints whom we met in Chapters 6 and 7 (Marguerite Bourgeoys and Marie Marguerite d'Youville) and nine blesseds. We devoted two chapters to two of the blesseds (André Bessette and Marie Rose Durocher). Here are brief profiles of the other seven:

François de Laval, born April 30, 1623 in Montigny-sur-Avre, France, was ordained a priest on May 1, 1647. He was named vicar apostolic of New France and consecrated a bishop on December 8, 1658. He arrived in Quebec on June 16, 1659 to organize the Catholic Church in Canada. When, in 1674, the apostolic vicarage of New France became the Diocese of Quebec, the first diocese north of Mexico, he became its bishop. His jurisdiction extended over all French-claimed territory in the New World.

He continued as Bishop of Quebec until his death on May 6, 1708 at the age of 85. Pope John Paul II beatified him on June 22, 1980. His feast is May 6.

Marie of the Incarnation was born Marie Guyard Martin on October 28, 1599 in Tours, France. She married and was widowed before she joined the Ursuline Nuns. She immigrated to Canada in 1639 and became the first superior of the Ursulines in Quebec. She was a missionary to the Indians and a writer. Pope John Paul II beatified her on June 22, 1980 along with François Laval. Her feast is April 30.

Marie Leonie Paradis was born Alodia Virginia Paradis on May 12, 1840 in L'Acadie, Quebec. She entered the convent of the Marianites of Holy Cross at Saint Laurent when she was fourteen and was admitted to religious profession in 1857. She taught for several years until she was asked by Father Camille Lefebvre to go to New Brunswick to direct the young Acadians serving at the College of Memramcook. There she founded the Institute of the Little Sisters of the Holy Family, dedicated to the service of priests. In 1895, upon the request of Bishop Paul LaRocque of Sherbrooke, the community was transferred there. At the time of Mother Leonie's death on May 3, 1912, the Little Sisters of the Holy Family served in forty houses in Canada and the United States. Pope John Paul II beatified her on September 11, 1984 during a visit to Canada.

Louis-Zephirin Moreau was born on April 1, 1824 in Bécancour, Quebec, the fifth child in a family of thirteen children. He was ordained to the priesthood in Montreal in 1846 at the age of 22. When the Diocese of Montreal was divided in 1852 and a new diocese was established in Saint Hyacinthe, Father Moreau accompanied the new bishop there. After serving three bishops for 23 years, he was appointed the fourth Bishop of Saint Hyacinthe in 1876. He served in that capacity until his death on May 24, 1901. Pope John Paul II beatified him in 1987. His feast is May 24.

Frederic Janssoone was born on November 19, 1838 in Ghyvelde, French Flanders, son of Pierre-Antoine Janssoone and Isabelle Bollengier. He joined the Franciscan Order and was ordained a priest on August 17, 1870. From 1876 to 1888 he served in the Holy Land as Vicar Custodial. He became a missionary in Canada in 1888 and was well known as a preacher, writer, and confessor. He died on August 4, 1916 in Montreal and Pope John Paul II beatified him on September 25, 1988.

Maria Catherine of Saint Augustine was born Catherine de Longpre on May 3, 1632. She joined the Sisters of Mercy and was known for her care of the sick and the poor. She died when she was 36 on May 8, 1668. Pope John Paul II beatified her on April 23, 1989.

Dina Belanger was born in Quebec City on April 30, 1897. Very gifted as a musician, she spent two years completing her studies at the Conservatory in New York City, returning to Quebec in 1918. She gave concerts for three years before her entrance into the novitiate of the Religious of Jesus and Mary at Sillery, Quebec. After her religious profession she gave music lessons. She died on September 4, 1929 when she was 32. Pope John Paul II beatified her on March 20, 1993.

For Mexico, we have already met Blessed Juan Diego and the 26 martyrs of the twentieth century. Here are other Mexican saints:

José María de Yermo y Parres was born on November 10, 1851 in Jalmolonga. He was ordained a priest for the Diocese of Leon on August 24, 1879. One day, after happening upon a gruesome scene of some pigs devouring the bodies of two abandoned newborn babies, he started a home for the poor and abandoned. With four women, he founded the Sacred Heart Shelter. This was also the start of the Servants of the Sacred Heart of Jesus and of the Poor. He went on to found schools, hospitals, nursing homes, orphanages and a home for rehabilitating women. Shortly before his death on September 20, 1904 he took his religious family to the difficult mission among the Tarahumara Indians in northern Mexico. Pope John Paul II beatified him on May 6, 1990 and canonized him on May 21, 2000.

María de Jesus Sacramentado was born María Natividad Venegas de la Torre on September 8, 1868 in Zaplotanejo, Jalisco.

She joined a community of pious women who ran a small hospital for the poor and in 1921 was elected superior. Bishop Miguel de la Mora invited her to write the Constitutions for a real religious community, which she did, and founded the Congregation of the Daughters of the Sacred Heart. Despite the persecution of the Church during the 1920s, the congregation succeeded. She served as superior of the congregation until 1954 and spent her last years in prayer and meditation. She died on July 30, 1959. Pope John Paul II beatified her on November 22, 1992 and canonized her on May 21, 2000.

Besides Juan Diego and Miguel Pro, Mexico has six other blesseds. The earliest was **Brother Sebastian of Aparicio**, who was born January 20, 1502 in Gudena, Spain. He was 31 when he set sail for Mexico in 1533. When he arrived, he realized that the Spanish colonists were hampered by a lack of roads, so he spent much of his life building roads. He became a Franciscan at age seventy. He died on February 25, 1600 and Pope Pius VI beatified him on May 27, 1790. His feast is February 25.

Blessed Anthony and John Christoforo were two adolescent brothers who were martyred in 1527 and 1529. Pope John Paul II beatified them on May 6, 1990.

Rafael Guizzar Valencia was born on April 26, 1878 and served as Bishop of Vera Cruz. He died on July 6, 1938. Pope John Paul II beatified him on January 29, 1995.

Elías del Soccorso Nieves was another martyr during the persecution of the Church in the 1920's. He was born on September 21, 1882 in Yuriria and was ordained a priest in the Order of Saint Augustine. He was martyred on March 10, 1928 and Pope John Paul II beatified him on October 12, 1997.

María Vincenza of Saint Dorothy was born Vincenza Chavez Orozco on February 6, 1867. She was the foundress of the Congregation of the Daughters of the Holy Trinity and of the Poor. She died in Guadalajara on July 30, 1949 and Pope John Paul II beatified her on November 9, 1997.

Although they didn't die in Mexico, that country can claim

fifteen other martyrs who have been canonized or beatified. They died in Japan during the persecution there at the end of the six-teenth century and the beginning of the seventeenth.

Saint Philip of Jesus de las Casas was the first native saint of the Americas to be canonized when Pope Pius IX did so in 1862. He was born in Mexico City on May 1, 1572 and became a Franciscan missionary to Japan. He was the first of 26 martyrs, under the leadership of Paul Miki, to die for their faith in Nagasaki, Japan. They were killed with spears as they hung on crosses on February 5, 1597. Saint Philip is the patron saint of Mexico City. His feast, together with the other martyrs of Nagasaki, is February 6.

Mexico can also claim four other companions of Paul Miki. Although they were not natives of Mexico, they resided there for a time. They are **Saints Peter Baptist Blasquez, Martin de Aguirre, Francis Blanco,** and **Francis de San Miguel**.

In 1867 Pope Pius IX beatified 205 martyrs who were among 40,000 who died for the faith in Japan between 1614 and 1640. Among them were these men who, although not native Mexicans, were missionaries there before going on to Japan: **Richard Trouve of St. Ann, Peter de Avila, Vincent Ramirez de San José, Peter Manrique de Zuniga, Louis Flores, Louis Sotelo, Louis Sasada, Louis Baba, Bartholomew Laurel Dias,** and **Bartholomew Gutierrez.**

Two countries in the Caribbean Sea, Cuba and the Dominican Republic, can claim saints.

Anthony Mary Claret has been called the "spiritual father of Cuba." He is not known primarily for his work in Cuba, though, because he was there for only six of his very eventful 62 years. He was born on Christmas Eve, 1807 at Sallent in Catalonia, northern Spain, the fifth of the eleven children of Juan Claret and Josepha Clara. He was ordained at age 28 and became well known as an outstanding preacher. He also wrote 144 books and founded the Religious Publishing House. In less than a century, eleven million copies of his books were distributed.

Father Claret founded the Missionary Sons of the Immaculate Heart of Mary, now known as the Claretians, when he was 42. Less than one month later, though, he was appointed archbishop of the much-neglected Archdiocese of Santiago, Cuba. He began its reform by stamping out concubinage among the priests, rectifying 9,000 marriages, and distributing 100,000 copies of a catechism he wrote. He made enemies through his efforts at reform and survived an attempt on his life when an assassin slashed open his face and wrist.

After six years in Cuba, Archbishop Claret was recalled to Madrid, Spain to be Father Confessor to the queen. In the revolution of 1868 he fled with the queen's party to Paris. He attended the First Vatican Council and spoke forcefully in favor of papal infallibility. He died on October 24, 1870, two days after the council adjourned. Pope Pius XI beatified him on February 25, 1934 and Pope Pius XII canonized him on May 7, 1950. His feast is October 23.

Ezequiel Moreño y Diaz is the saint from the Dominican Republic. He was born on April 9, 1848 and became a member of the Augustinian Recollects Order. He was bishop of Pasto in the Dominican Republic. He died on August 19, 1906 in Monteagudo. Pope Paul VI beatified him on November 1, 1975 and Pope John Paul II canonized him on October 11, 1992.

In Central America, Guatemala has one blessed. **Pedro de San José Betancur** was born May 16, 1619 in Tenerife, Canary Islands. He became a lay member of the Third Order of Saint Francis and founded the Bethlehemite Brothers and Sisters. He arrived in Guatemala in 1651 and established a hospital, school and homes for the poor. He died on April 25, 1667. Pope John Paul II beatified him on June 22, 1980. His feast is April 25.

In South America, Argentina has no saints but two blesseds:

Laura Vicuna was born on April 5, 1891 in Chile and was only twelve years old when she died on January 22, 1904 in Junin de los Andes. Pope John Paul II beatified her on September 3, 1988.

Nazaria Ignazia March Mesa was born on January 10, 1889

in Madrid. She was foundress of the Congregation of the Missionary Crusaders of the Church. She died in Buenos Aires on July 6, 1943. Pope John Paul II beatified her on September 27, 1992. Brazil also has no saints, but 33 blesseds.

André de Soveral, Ambrosio Francisco Ferro and 28 companions are the most recent blesseds. They were priests and lay men and women killed by Brazilian Indians and Dutch soldiers during the Dutch occupation of northeastern Brazil in 1645. Some of them were killed on July 16 of that year in Cunhau and the others on October 3 in Uruacu. The martyrs included a dozen children and several married couples who were the first native-born Brazilians to be beatified. Father Soveral was also Brazilian while Father Ferro was Portuguese. Pope John Paul II beatified them on March 5, 2000.

José de Anchieta was one of the early missionaries to Brazil. Born on March 19, 1534, he was ordained a Jesuit priest. He died on July 9, 1597 in Reritiba, Brazil and Pope John Paul II beatified him on July 22, 1980.

Paolina of the Dying Heart of Jesus was born Amabile Visenteiner on December 16, 1865 in Vattaro-Trent, Italy. She was the foundress of the Little Sisters of the Immaculate Conception. She died on July 9, 1942 in São Paulo and Pope John Paul II beatified her on October 18, 1991.

Antonio of Saint Ann was born Antonio Galvão de Franca in 1739. He was a professed priest of the Discalced Franciscans and founder of the Monastery of the Conceptionist Sisters. He died on December 23, 1822 and Pope John Paul II beatified him on October 25, 1998.

Chile has one saint and one blessed:

Teresa Fernandez Solar is known as Saint Teresa of the Andes. She was born on July 13, 1900 in Santiago del Chile and died at age 22 while a Discalced Carmelite novice on April 12, 1923 in Los Andes. Pope John Paul II beatified her on April 3, 1987 and canonized her on March 21, 1993.

Alberto Hurtado Cruchaga was born on January 22, 1901

at Viña del Mar. He was a Jesuit priest. He died on August 8, 1952 in Santiago del Chile. Pope John Paul II beatified him on October 16, 1994.

Colombia has one saint, Peter Claver (see Chapter 3) and two blesseds:

Maria of the Incarnation (easily confused with Canada's Blessed Marie of the Incarnation) was born Vincenza Rosal on October 27, 1815 in Quelzatenango. She reformed the Bethlehemite Sisters and died on August 24, 1886 in Fulcan. Pope John Paul II beatified her on May 4, 1997.

Mariano of Jesus Euse Hoyos was born on October 14, 1845 in Yarumal. He was a diocesan priest. He died on July 12, 1926 at Angostura. Pope John Paul II beatified him on April 9, 2000.

Ecuador has two saints and one blessed:

Mariana of Jesus Paredes y Flores, known as "the Lily of Quito," is almost an exact counterpart of Saint Rose of Lima. She was born on October 31, 1618 in Quito a year after Saint Rose's death. She was a lay woman known for her holiness, her severe penances, and her work for the poor and sick. She died on May 26, 1645 when she was only 27. Pope Pius IX beatified her on November 20, 1853 and Pope John Paul II canonized her on July 9, 1950. She is the patroness of Ecuador. Her feast is May 28.

Miguel Febres Cordero was born on November 7, 1854. He became a Christian Brother and was renowned as an educator. He died on February 9, 1910 at Premia del Mar. Pope Paul VI beatified him on October 30, 1977 and Pope John Paul II canonized him on October 21, 1984.

Mercedes of Jesus was born Mercedes Molina in 1828. She was the foundress of the Institute of the Sisters of Blessed Mariana of Jesus, which she founded after Saint Mariana was beatified. She died on June 12, 1883. Pope John Paul II beatified her on February 1, 1985.

Paraguay has three saints who were martyred on November 16, 1828 by Indians. **Roque (or Roch) Gonzalez, Alphonse**

Rodriguez, and John de Castillo were Jesuit missionaries who worked in the Indian mission settlements (called reductions). An Indian chief named Carupe, instigated by the tribe's witch doctor, Nezu, led a war party that killed the three missionaries. Pope Pius XI beatified them on January 28, 1934 and Pope John Paul II canonized them on May 16, 1988.

Peru has two blesseds in addition to the five saints we met in Chapter 2:

Anna of the Angels Monteagudo was a professed Dominican nun, born around the year 1600 in Arequipa. She died on January 10, 1686, also in Arequipa. Pope John Paul II beatified her on February 2, 1985.

Narcisa of Jesus Martillo Moran was a laywoman, born in 1833 on Nobol. She died on December 8, 1869 in Lima. Pope John Paul II beatified her on October 25, 1992.

Uruguay has one blessed, **María Frances of Jesus**, who was born Anna María Rubatto on February 14, 1844 in Carmagnola. She was the foundress of the Capuchin Tertiary Sisters of Loano. She died on August 6, 1904 in Montevideo. Pope John Paul II beatified her on October 10, 1993.

Venezuela has one blessed, **María of Saint Joseph**, who was born Laura Alvarado Cardozo on April 25, 1875 in Choron. She was the foundress of the Augustinian Recollect Sisters of the Heart of Jesus. She died on April 2, 1967 in Maracay. Pope John Paul II beatified her on May 7, 1995.

ST PAULS